SAME LIGHT, MANY CANDLES

Working with Vulnerable Children and Mothers Within Toxically Stressed Communities

Carol Cole

Same Light Many Candles

© 2017 Carol Cole

ISBN: 978-1-936849-40-6

Author: Carol Cole
Publications Coordinator: Donna Lee Miele
Copy Editor: Bill Day
Cover Art and illustrations: Sharry Wright
Graphic Design: Calliope Creative – Jennifer Siegrist

Published in the United States by
The Waldorf Early Childhood Association of North America
285 Hungry Hollow Road
Spring Valley, NY 10977
www.waldorfearlychildhood.org

Visit our online store at *store.waldorfearlychildhood.org*

This publication is made possible through a grant from
the Waldorf Curriculum Fund.

WECAN
WALDORF EARLY CHILDHOOD
ASSOCIATION OF NORTH AMERICA

For the children

To Evie

With love from me & your brother,

Carol

November, 2017

Contents

A Note on the Cover Drawing

The festival of the Advent spiral is an image of the path to light, both inner and outer. A spiral, often made of evergreens, moss, or straw and flowers is laid on the ground. At the center of the spiral is a large lit candle. While Christmas carols are sung or played, each child or adult, one at a time, carries an unlit candle, intent on finding a way to the center. Upon reaching the center, each one lights his or her candle from the large light and then leaves it along the path, helping to light the way for the next person. The room, at first illuminated by just the one large candle, slowly brightens through each individual's effort. I have celebrated this dignifying act of finding the light and leaving one's own light along the path in many settings, including the Waldorf kindergarten, Camphill school, with children from the township in South Africa, with mothers and children at Raphael homeless shelter, and with children and adults at Sophia Project.

Celebrating together in this way has brought a shared experience of the profound significance of individual and community, of beauty, and of hope. As it has for so many others, including Dr. Karl König, it inspires me. It has also helped me double my efforts in times that seemed overwhelmingly difficult. For these reasons, I have chosen the ennobling, encouraging, healing image of the Advent spiral, beautifully drawn by Sharry Wright, for the cover of this book.

Acknowledgements

My heartfelt thanks to:

Robert McDermott—friend, chair of Sophia Project Board of Trustees, professor, and author—for his encouragement, guidance, and assistance every step of the way on this writing adventure.

Sharry Wright for capturing the mood of simple beauty and peace in her drawings, and for her keen insights.

Patricia Kenney-Schliebe and Ellie Wood for reading drafts and listening with kindness to my worries.

Donna Miele and everyone at WECAN Publications for their patience and support.

My family for being a continuous source of strength.

My husband David for his unconditional love and his willingness to do whatever is needed.

Foreword 1:
A Venture into the Social Needs of Our Time

Strength, Commitment, and Grace

It was with great excitement and joy that I learned of the Sophia Project. A truly bold, really new initiative arising out of the Camphill impulse and working into an urgent social need of our time!

I made my first visit in the early days when the childcare was a part of Raphael Homeless Shelter in San Francisco. I visited later at Sophia House in West Oakland, and came again after the acquisition of Myrtle House. These visits were deeply impressive, and increasingly so as I witnessed the strength, commitment, and grace with which this impulse developed. The deepening achievement, the growing well-being of the children and the joy and commitment of the coworkers—young and old—were so compelling. What were the sources that nourished the health and vitality of this extraordinary development?

Care of the Soul

Before Camphill began, Rudolf Steiner gave an intriguing indication of the scope of the healing work that could arise out of anthroposophy. He rejected the name proposed for the first home for children with developmental delays and disabilities; they should choose a name that does not stamp the children immediately! Don't start with a label, put the child first. He dictated: "Children in need of care of the soul." And with this, the future centers of curative education had received their name. In Britain this became "children in need of special care."

In our time, who is not in need of human recognition, special care, interest, and understanding? Who does not need to be seen and addressed on the level of their true humanness, their life of soul? Echoing Karl König, we may well ask: "Who is not in need of healing in our time?"

A Place of Human Striving

Camphill began with some clear intentions: to build a community where the ideals and insights of anthroposophy would not only be studied but were to be practiced, embodied, applied to daily life. This would be a community-building activity flowing from each person's total humanity. If the group were to strive for this high ideal, they would be perpetually "on the way" and would create a living, truly social, healing environment for all who lived there. It was to be a community that continually worked to understand more deeply, uphold, and nurture the true human being in its threefoldness of body, soul and spirit. This community dedicated to perpetual and deepening human development would develop social forms that would meet these differentiated needs.

To Gain Once More Their Human Dignity

The refugee was an image that underlay the work of Camphill. The founders were themselves refugees and felt a deep affinity with the children who came to live with them. The children were seen as refugees of another sort, longing for social inclusion and human understanding. Karl König spoke about curative education in a broad, humanly universal way as a necessary response to deteriorating social conditions, processes of dehumanization. Its impulse to make a home, a shelter, a safe, nurturing, inspiring place for all those for whom society simply couldn't or wouldn't provide; to create a place where the individual was truly seen, and encouraged to unfold and become; to celebrate the uniqueness of human life in all its glorious diversity, based on the conviction of the eternal, inviolable spiritual core, that divine potential existing within each and every human being.

Camphill began in Scotland with children in need of special care. These children had, notably, developmental delays, physical and educational disabilities. Other children joined who were socially deprived and maladjusted. Later, the work expanded to village communities where adults with special needs were engaged in meaningful life and work. There were activities with young offenders and work projects with prisoners; another project began to work with people with drug addiction; another with people with mental illness; and yet another for war refugees. Still, other tasks lay hidden in the lap of the future.

Beauty, Goodness, and Strength

The Sophia Project brought the UR-Camphill impulse to West Oakland. What a wonderful work they undertook! The children were enveloped in a mantle of warmth and security. It was like entering a secret garden, a magical kingdom, full of peace, beauty, goodness and love. The children were seen and they were supported. They were nurtured in body, soul and spirit. There were moments when some were able to gain access to an experience that was essentially their birthright—the innocence of childhood.

The children greeted me, a stranger, with open-hearted trust and enthusiasm. I remember on one visit being deeply moved as the clean-up before nap time took place. All the precious toys were gathered together and put away in their proper place. And there was a proper place for everything. Then I watched the children as they worked in pairs with such earnest concentration and care, neatly folding the silken veils of many colors with which they had made their playhouses. How important that these children experience the value of creating order out of chaos, of caring for each toy, each block, of being conscious and responsible for things.

The children had little cots for their nap time. They napped under their very own, handmade quilts. When they aged out of the program, the quilt went home with them. Something so beautiful, precious, handmade, enduring and their very own!

And birthday parties! Now these were impressive events! The mothers were invited to attend and watched with awe at the ceremony in which their child was truly lifted out, honored, acknowledged, celebrated. There were presents and songs, and a special verse or poem and of course, cake!

The young coworkers were deeply engaged, profoundly committed, responsible and conscientious, ably guided and accompanied by David and Carol. They clearly had profound respect for the work of the Sophia Project and gratitude that they were allowed to be part of it.

Amongst the whole community of coworkers there was mutual support, deep gratitude for each other and dedication to the task that they were undertaking together. They were aware of the nearly holy aspect of their tasks with the children, which they approached with awe and reverence. Their love for the project and the children shone!

Ethical Transitioning

David and Carol realized that they could not carry on forever and that their successors were not yet ready to take over the project. I have never known of such a conscientious transition! With the greatest concern, love and care and an extraordinary sense of responsibility for each and every child that had been in the program, they planned and executed a many-staged and deeply ethical transition. They remained inwardly committed to each of the relationships that they had made and retained interest and engagement with all of those children and families who needed or wanted it.

How Good That This Work Has Begun

The Sophia Project has been an inspiration to so many and has literally transformed the lives of the children and families in its care. Through this work seeds for future developments have surely been planted in thinking hearts!

Wanda Root
Camphill Village, Copake

Foreword II:
Being Human in Our Time

In this inspiring book, Carol Cole explains that celebrating festivals together enabled the Sophia Project community to experience the profound significance of the individual and the community. This story of the Sophia Project reveals the enduring wisdom that lives within each human soul and finds expression through living deeds. This is also a story about creating nurturing programs for young children and mothers at risk of recurring homelessness. The story is an answer to the problem of homelessness in our time.

Carol's life work with young children and their mothers in the United States and South Africa has been dedicated to finding the light in the face of increasing darkness, and leaving light along that path. The Sophia Project has been a life-defining deed. The image of the advent festival on the book's cover illustrates the beauty and hope that the founders of Sophia Project carried for fifteen years, first in the two Sophia Project houses in West Oakland, California and later in San Rafael, California.

Trust and openness were crucial to the community that the founders located in West Oakland. They selected this location for the first house because services were sparse and rents affordable. Being in West Oakland required the community to meet the challenges of a low-income, often violent neighborhood. Mindfulness, consistency, and respectful behavior were essential for safety and were often returned in kind. Once the neighbors were convinced that Sophia Project would care for children, they responded kindly, saying, "We will pass the word."

All those involved in establishing the new facility realized that the beauty of nature would signal new life and hope. While painting and repairing the house, volunteers also created a front garden with lavender and honeysuckle. Giant sunflowers astounded the children who delighted in picking bouquets for their mothers.

Four years after acquiring the first house, a gift enabled the purchase of a second property within walking distance to Sophia House. Myrtle House was not occupied by families who would be displaced, rather it was used as a transient drug house. It was affordable and large enough to house coworkers and the infant/toddler program.

Without the dedication of the board of trustees, led by board chair Robert McDermott, the work of Sophia Project would not have been possible. In addition to collaborating with Carol and David on the legal, financial, and strategic responsibilities, board members carried in their hearts and minds the goals, principles, and daily work of the project.

The core of Sophia Project was most evidenced in the daily, weekly, monthly, and yearly cycle of programs carried by a tiny band of long-term coworkers and interns. The interns received room and board, health insurance, and a modest stipend, and were nourished by a strong in-service training and monthly counseling. They developed inner resourcefulness and brought emotional health and physical stamina to the daily work. These warriors of the heart knew that their inner resources and outer skills were in service to the children and mothers.

As stated in Chapter 3 of this book, the project's goal was "to alleviate and, to the extent possible, reverse the developmental delays and extreme emotional fragility of children who had suffered the traumatic effects of deep poverty, violence, and homelessness." The program's education and development activities were based on Rudolf Steiner's early childhood indications tailored to meet the needs of these particular children. Coworkers protected, guided, and encouraged the children's imaginative play. As the children developed relationships to the world around them, they and their mothers steadily replaced the feeling of isolation with the experience of connection. They were able to say: "We belong here."

Programs supported both the children and their mothers. In this book Carol refers to a study by the Harvard University Center of the Developing Child that identified several "effectiveness factors" concerning children from low- and very-low-income families. All of these factors were part of the Sophia programs, including the combination of high quality early childhood education with family support services.

As Carol states in her introduction to this book, not one of the 112 children from the forty-eight families served by the Sophia Project has returned to homelessness. In addition, Sophia Project served dozens of neighborhood children who were not a part of the formal programs. After fifteen years, 98% of the families served remain healthy and stable. All of the children who were a part of the early childhood programs have gone on to participate well in school. They are joyful and engaged.

These numbers represent a mighty deed, one that defies the accepted expectation of failure and hopelessness faced by each single-mother, low-income family striving to raise children while threatened by homelessness.

The ideals and personal stories of the founders and coworkers, as well as the biographies of some of the families served by Sophia Project, provide an insight into what it means to be a human being in our time.

High idealism, compassion, kindness, joy, and above all, love, when put into practice become everyday virtues, become deeds that heal and transform both the practitioners and those they strive to serve.

This is what happened at Sophia Project for fifteen years.

This has been a living deed inscribed into life for all time.

This is what "home" looks like.

Ann Stahl
Faculty, Sunbridge Institute
Waldorf Early Childhood Teacher Education, 1992-2016

Introduction

The biography of Sophia Project is richly interwoven with ideals, organizations, and personal biographies that together make an integrated whole. Located in a low-income neighborhood in Oakland, California, Sophia Project (1998–2014, then continuing informally for several additional years) served children and mothers at risk of recurring homelessness. This work drew primarily on the insights and practices of Waldorf early childhood education and Camphill community life. The name Sophia Project invoked our wish and our intention to be guided by Sophia, a being called by many names including Wisdom, and alive with qualities that include love and compassion.

After giving several inspiring examples of Sophia through time, Christopher Bamford, in *An Endless Trace*, explains that these different images of Sophia—the way of Wisdom—show the need to avoid rendering Sophia literally. Rather, we must understand Sophia/Wisdom as an activity which we can embody and participate in. "Mary" has always been the guiding image for this. Bamford writes,

> Mary stands for virtues like faith, kindness, compassion, purity, humility, inner attentiveness, joy, sincerity, patience, and the ability to wait and to hold in active openhearted receptivity. She embodied them in the midst of a long daily life that stretched from birth and childhood, through the experience of the Incarnation, to her last earthly days in Ephesus with the beloved disciple, John.[1]

At Sophia Project we strove to practice these virtues while implementing the ideals and methods of Waldorf education and Camphill community life. This approach to the work presupposed and in turn deepened the dignity and healing resources of each child and mother. The effects within the neighborhood and among all those involved have endured long past the formal close of the project.

This book is the story of how transformative healing was brought forth from a wise approach to education and a dedicated live-in staff. The story began and was sustained by the project's response to the needs of these children and families. The work was based on the conviction that the wisdom of Rudolf Steiner and Karl König reveal profound insights for the creation of community that enables individuals—children, mothers, and coworkers—to heal, strengthen, and build necessary capacities.[2]

It is widely acknowledged by donors, granting founders, and visitors that Sophia Project has realized profound results. It served 112 children enrolled in the daily infant/toddler program, early childhood program, the before-and-after-school program, and the weekend programs. It also served dozens of neighborhood children. All of the children who were a part of the early childhood programs have gone on to participate well in school. They are joyful, engaged, and working to the best of their abilities. Their teachers have regularly commented on the social skills, harmony, and compassion the children have brought to their classrooms and wider community.

This outcome continues to be true thirteen years after the first children graduated from the early childhood program. As of February 2017, most of the children attend inner-city public middle schools and high schools; eighteen have received grants to attend parochial schools. More remarkably, fifteen of the children are in college and many families have a small savings fund for their children's college in the future. All of these children are able to perform well both academically and socially because of their own developmental health and because their families remain stable.

Not one of the 48 families served by Sophia Project has returned to homelessness. After fifteen years, 98 percent of our families remain healthy and stable. Armed with new self-esteem from their time at Sophia Project, most of the mothers have been able to bring compassion and order into the harsh, chaotic communities in which they live. We have joyfully observed many of the mothers bringing festival celebrations to their communities. Their neighbors have been encouraged to attempt change in their own daily lives as they witnessed the transformation the mothers have brought to their families through simple (but hard-won) nourishing daily practices such as dinner together or story time in the children's early years. In these ways and others the mothers themselves have brought much-needed social renewal to their own communities.

Essentially this book can be seen as a description of the conditions created to support healing in the following true story.

~

Paula

When Sophia Project programs opened, Paula[3] was two and a half years old. Her mother, Kelly, came to the door of Sophia House with her two young daughters, Paula and her four-year-old sister Pollie. "Can you take this one?" Kelly asked, pointing to Paula, "It's too late for the other one." When respectfully asked later in the conversation why it was too late for Pollie, she explained that Pollie was already a lost cause, damaged, ill-behaved, and rough. In her estimation, the "Baby still has a chance," meaning a chance to not repeat the discouraging cycle of inner and outer poverty.

Kelly was being pragmatic. Her experiences in life led her to expect that Pollie's course was set; Pollie would likely have a life much like her mother's. Kelly did not want this for Pollie anymore than she wanted it for Paula; it was simply inevitable. At best, she hoped Pollie would be able to avoid some of the more painful events she herself had experienced. Kelly had her first child more than a decade before Pollie and Paula were born. She was only fourteen years old, her first child a product of rape. She had barely begun 9th grade when she became pregnant. She did not return to school and never completed her GED. Like many of the Sophia House mothers, her early life had repeated incidents of incest, physical abuse, and neglect. She struggled with debilitating mental health issues. Kelly had spent time in jail for petty theft and she had been homeless. She lived three blocks from Sophia House in a crowded, frequently violent apartment. The following chapters explain both Kelly and her family's need for sustained relationship within a nurturing community and Kelly's increasing belief in metamorphosis. Pollie did, of course, come to Sophia House and her story will be also be related.

With this background, the following short depictions of Paula's life demonstrate the need to nourish and protect Paula and all children, thereby providing them the opportunity to develop capacities needed for a safe, warm, engaged, and fulfilling life.

Paula at almost 3 years old:

> Fearful and frantic, Paula arrived each morning cold and hungry. She was very thin; she ate very little, quickly stuffing small amounts in her mouth. Her teeth were rotted to the gums. She cried frequently. Hyper-vigilant, she almost never played. Sometimes it is difficult to believe that a child can recover from constant trauma during the first years of life but as can be seen below, even deep scars of violence and fear can be healed. Paula came to Sophia House twelve hours a day, five days a week for three years in the early childhood program, for several more years in the before-and-after-school program, and continued as needed in the family support program.

Paula at almost 4 years old:

Standing in the garden at Sophia House, Paula was excited that she could for the first time hear and see a bird singing. She had become peaceful enough to be able to notice a bird outside. She asked, "Who is it singing for?" She was told the bird's song is for everyone. "Even for me?" she asked incredulously. Many young children report that the moon is following them. By contrast the Sophia House children needed careful guidance to the recognition that the sun shines for us all, not just for those it likes, and that the bird's song is free for everyone. This phenomenon points to the children's deep sense of not belonging, of not having a place.

Paula at almost 8 years old:

Gradually, as Paula had more time in the early childhood program, she began to feel safe, to trust, and to eat. With time and guidance she began to play and make her own connections to nature, arts, story, stars, moon, and sun. She won a grant to attend a local Catholic elementary school and came to Sophia House before and after school. One evening she spontaneously wrote the following poem:

I'm glad I'm me. I'm glad I'm me
There is no one else I want to be.
I'm happy I'm the person who can do the things that I can do.

If I were someone else
Then I would feel strange
I'd wonder why.
I'm positive that I'd be sad
But I am me and I am glad.

Foundations and some donors are intensely interested in quantitative measurements and reporting of progress. The section in this book on assessment addresses this need. However, sometimes the most dramatic piece of evidence comes about spontaneously—a picture, a poem, an interaction—impossible to replicate and difficult to measure. Like the children's physical growth, all of a sudden they are looking very different than they did six months earlier. So, too, with interior growth and healing. Every day they come to heal, and then suddenly a child writes a poem that says it all—"I'm glad I'm me."

Paula, 14 years old, her high school application essay:

> *If I could change one thing in my community it would be the violence and the lack of safety. In my neighborhood it is very loud and I can often hear gunshot. Recently there was a robbery at the nearby gas station. The man ran down our street and into the neighbor's house. He said he had a bomb so the police blocked off the street. There was not a bomb in the house, but the police didn't catch the guy so he was still free and he could go into any house. I was afraid for myself and for my neighbors.*

> *The violence bothers me because everyone feels scared. The kids play in the street and they see violence and people doing drugs. This can influence them to do the same thing. Then they grow up to be criminals and the community gets even worse. Even though people in my community struggle with other issues like not having enough food, keeping a job, and poverty in general, I know violence makes everything worse.*

> *From the time I was two years old until 7th grade, I had an example of non-violence in my neighborhood. I went to Sophia House. Sophia House was an all day and sometimes nighttime child-care house. I felt safe there. I learned how to be non-violent and how to share and cooperate. Sophia House was a second home to me. They are a second family for me.*

One of the reasons I want to attend ND is because it is also a safe environment. It is a small community and everyone feels safe, free to know each other, and inspired to learn. I hope one day I can help to bring change to my community and make it a better place for people.

~

At the time of this writing (February 2017), Paula is 17 years old and a senior at the Catholic high school for which she wrote the above essay. She has been on the varsity basketball team since she was a freshman, she has a 3.7 GPA, and she participates in musical productions. Three universities have offered her early acceptance. She hopes some day to work in the mental health field within her community.

The following pages describe the community, programs, support, and practices that created the necessary conditions to help bring about Paula's well being and that of the other 111 children and their mothers.

My husband David Barlow and I cofounded and lived at Sophia Project. In addition to working in the programs David was responsible for building operations including renovations, and financial administration. I served as executive director and was responsible for the programs and for coworker education. The Camphill-inspired, live-in community of long-term coworkers and interns created a vessel within which the children and mothers became well. To support the work, an effective intern and coworker training program was developed. More than thirty interns worked with and received training at Sophia Project; many have continued to work in organizations committed to serving vulnerable children and families. Sophia Project was the first satellite site for the first two years of the BA in curative education offered through Camphill Special School, School of Curative Education, now the Camphill Academy.

Collaborative working was developed with Raphael House Family Shelter, Child Protective Services, Oakland Unified School District, and Oakland's Children's Hospital. Sophia Project served as the family liaison for Habitat for Humanity, which has enabled six of the families to own their own home. Several foundations referred other agencies to Sophia Project to learn "best practices" in this work.

Sophia Project was associated with the Waldorf Early Childhood Association of North America and was an affiliate of the Camphill Association of North America.

Wider community recognition included an award as one of five East Bay projects to receive the "Local Hero Award for Neighborhood Renewal" by the Bank of America in 2005. Sophia Project was also chosen by the Whole Child Initiative as one of 12 effective models worldwide serving disadvantaged young children. I presented the work at the State of the World Forum, September 2000, convened in cooperation with the United Nations.

It is important to have the work recognized, but what is primary, fundamental, and essential is the hard-won, awe-inspiring transformation accomplished by the children and mothers we served. Before coming to Sophia Project, these families had experienced despair and a loss of human dignity through homelessness, violence, abuse, poverty and sustained high levels of fear. Put succinctly, they are now well, and they have become agents of change by living compassionate, healthy lives.

Special insights and conditions are necessary for such transformations to take place. In most cases the children and mothers were part of the daily programs for three years, and then were a part of the family support program in which participation decreased in intensity over the following three to five years. Daily programs included infant /toddler development, early childhood education, and before-and-after-school programs. Weekend programs included respite care, festival celebrations, outings, and artistic activity days.

Some may say that the financial resources and level of skill needed to support this extent of transformation were excessive, or that it simply takes too much time. But the investment seems small when one considers the ripple effect of health and healing these families are able to bring into their communities. It is also important to bear in mind that the conditions that Sophia Project has addressed—hungry, frightened children, poor quality childcare, multigenerational abuse, and violent neighborhoods—have existed for many years. A comparatively short time is needed to create healing conditions that replace ignorance and lack of care with self-education and awareness of the needs of others; replace neglect with dedicated work; replace destruction of entire neighborhoods with supportive organizations.

The National Center for Children in Poverty reports that in the United States, "More than 1.5 million children live in families without a home. Among those, 42 percent are under the age of 6 . . . Homeless families are more likely to be led by a single mother in her twenties with young children."[4]

The multicultural population of children and mothers Sophia Project served fits into these disturbing statistics. Through the profound gifts of Waldorf early childhood education and Camphill community life, a deep and lasting transformation has taken place within these children and mothers and within their communities. This renewal brings healing in the present time and will positively affect future generations. The intention of this book is to share our experiences with those who are called to work with children in similar circumstances and to encourage those who do not see this as their own work to give ardent and inclusive support to those who attempt it. While there are certainly situations and communities that may not be suitable for this work, a vast number are suitable. We have the wisdom to effect positive change; there is an urgent need.

Although an understanding of the effects of homelessness and trauma are necessary for effective work with these children and mothers, this book is not a study of homelessness or traumatized children. Nor does it explain Waldorf early childhood education or Camphill principles. There are many readily available works on these topics.

Part One of this book is a narrative account of the life of the Sophia Project. Part Two contains documents central to the operation of the project, including sections on assessment, funding, and other documents referred to in Part One. True accounts that originally appeared in Sophia Project newsletters are reproduced in Part One.

Part One begins at Raphael House family homeless shelter in San Francisco, where David and I were employed as Operations Director and Director of Children's Services, respectively.

Endnotes

1. Christopher Bamford, *An Endless Trace: The Passionate Pursuit of Wisdom in the West* (New Paltz, NY: Codhill Press 2003), p. 27.

2. Some portions of this book appear in: Carol Cole and Robert McDermott, "Sophia Project," in the autumn/winter 2013, spring 2014, and summer 2014 issues of *Being Human*. Other portions of this book were first published in Sophia Project newsletters.

3. Throughout the book the names of children and mothers have been changed; their accounts are true.

4. Yumiko Aratani, "Homeless Children and Youth." *National Center for Children in Poverty*, September 2009. www.nccp.org/publications/pub_888.html.

Part One

From Seed, Flowering, to Seed

Chapter One:
*Beginnings**

In San Francisco, upstairs in the children's playroom of the Raphael House family homeless shelter, four-year-old Sammy has made a little house from large wooden play frames for the walls and a long rainbow cloth for the roof. While other children play noisily around her, she lays another cloth on the floor, crawls in and, lying on her back looking up at the rainbow roof, falls asleep. A few minutes later Sammy's young mother comes into the playroom. She sees Sammy sleeping peacefully, her eyes fill and then tears softly run down her cheeks. "She's asleep," she whispers softly. She goes out and quickly returns with several of the other mothers, their bittersweet smiles show their deep understanding and appreciation of what is taking place. The mothers quietly leave; Sammy stays asleep.

Sammy, like many of the children at the shelter, has experienced debilitating trauma stemming from homelessness, sexual abuse, physical abuse, fear, and hunger. She is hyper-vigilant, unable to trust, anxious for her safety, frantic that her mother or safe adult will disappear. Her behavior is erratic, sometimes wild and hysteric, more often silent and nervously watchful. This deep, constant, toxic fear thwarts healthy early childhood development and renders her unable, out of her own forces, to truly engage in play or exploration of the world around her.

Sammy sleeps only when overcome by exhaustion and then only when completely covered, scrunched in a corner with her mother's body close around her. Now, after many weeks of rhythm, beauty, play, and the gentle guidance of experienced teachers, she has made herself a little rainbow house and, inside, she peacefully sleeps.

It is wrenchingly painful that it is only on this one single occasion that the conditions surrounding Sammy have given her what she needs to feel safe enough to sleep. Now, under the right conditions, this vulnerable little girl begins to courageously overcome adversity and find her way to healing and to sleep. Sophia Project was created in response to the suffering and courage of Sammy and many other little children.

Sammy, our waif-like child with dark circles around her big dark eyes, straggly hair, and broken teeth, has a smile that, on the occasions it manages to break through, lights up the whole room and cheers the heart of everyone present. This smile is imprinted

---

*   These chapters are intelligible only if the introduction has been read.

on our souls and has anchored us in our core work of nourishing and protecting the light within each child. These little ones are building the very foundation upon which the rest of their lives will depend. They must somehow do so within the war zones many of our inner cities have become. Despite these oppressive, often shattering circumstances, enough freedom from overpowering fear must be created so these children can bring their gifts to the world. We were (and continue to be) convinced that with the insights of Waldorf early childhood work, Camphill community life, curative education, collaboration, and focused determination, it is possible to create conditions in which these children can heal and thrive.

The first practical step in creating Sophia Project was to work out an agreement with Raphael House, the first family homeless shelter established in San Francisco, directed at that time by Fr. David Lowell. The Raphael House live-in community was based on the teachings of the Russian Orthodox Church. With the help of an organizational development team from Stanford University, a three-year understanding was forged between Raphael House and Sophia Project. This understanding included the following five components:

David would continue for one year to direct operations at Raphael House.

I would continue for 3 years to direct Raphael House Children's Services.

Sophia Project would hold some festivals in common with Raphael House. These would be based at Sophia Project.

Sophia Project programs would give priority to Raphael House children and families.

Raphael House would financially support the program work at Sophia Project.

This collaboration between Raphael House and Sophia Project was an invaluable aid to Sophia Project in its first years and an inspiration to all who sustained it, and all who observed it.

David and I bought a how-to book on forming a nonprofit and, with phone help from the government filing office, filed for and were granted 501(c)(3) nonprofit status for Sophia Project, a public charity.

Skillfully led by Robert McDermott, the first and subsequent board of trustees was dedicated to the work of Sophia Project. Several board members volunteered weekly in the programs.[1] At each meeting, before the more traditional strategic, legal, and financial board work began, a report was given on the work with the children and mothers followed by a short educational explanation of the principles or methods underpinning the programs. Board members were always aware of the intention of the work, the anthroposophical, Camphill, and Waldorf principles informing the work, and the aspirations of the live-in community. At the beginning of board meetings we contemplated the following verse:

> The thought manifests as the word;
> The word manifests as the deed;
> The deed develops into habit;
> And habit hardens into character.
> So watch the thought and its ways with care,
> And let it spring from love
> Born out of concern for all beings.

> ~ Buddha, from Roberts and Amidon[2]

West Oakland

We chose to establish Sophia Project in West Oakland, across the bay from San Francisco, because existing services were sparse, and some Raphael House families had found affordable housing there after leaving the San Francisco shelter. West Oakland's population is primarily African-American; at one time it was the Black Panther Party's center of activity. While many people are aware of the political arm of the Black Panthers, fewer are aware of the social programs they operated, including free breakfast for children as well as several other nutrition, education, and healthcare programs. Tragically, this aspect of West Oakland was no longer easily visible and had all but disappeared, leaving a low-income, high-crime, gang- and drug-fueled violent neighborhood.

David and I spent some time driving around West Oakland looking for a house and had several false starts. We then heard of a house that was not on the market but whose owner, a victim of domestic violence, would consider selling to people addressing this issue. Driving by, we saw there was a bus in the driveway with extension cords going into the house. The house itself was filthy and ill kept, occupied by many transient young people. Affordable housing is scarce in the San Francisco Bay Area; it was important to us that we did not dislodge a family or anyone who considered the house their permanent home. Obviously it is perverse to make people homeless in order to create a place to provide services for children and families at risk of recurring homelessness.

Ellie Wood, a board member, provided the down payment for the first house, Sophia House, and five years later the second house, Myrtle House. Ellie is Sophia Project's steadfast and loving godmother. Over the years and in myriad ways she supported all aspects of the work; as of February 2017 she continues, as needed, to support the children and mothers. We obtained the Sophia House mortgage from the Rudolf Steiner Foundation at a competitive market rate. At that time mortgages from RSF were usually guaranteed by a community of people such as Waldorf parents or a Camphill community. The families we served were of course unable to provide such a guarantee; Ellie undersigned the loan from RSF.

Life in the Neighborhood

Moving In

From the outside, the house appeared too small but it turned out to be perfect, a three-story Victorian painted warm yellow with grass-green trim. The third floor was an attic that fifty years before had been living quarters but was now accessed by climbing a ladder, moving boards, and squeezing through a hole in the second-floor ceiling. The first renovation was to build a stairway to the third floor, demolish, and then reconstruct the rooms. After five months of hard and very creative work, this floor housed the large respite care room, three bedrooms, an office, and two bathrooms.[3] The ground floor became the nursery/kindergarten and childcare rooms. The second floor held bedrooms, community space, and the before-and-after-school program.

It was critical that all the bathrooms had good light, ideally daylight. Although sometimes expensive, it was crucial that the bathrooms not be dark, even before turning on a light. Much trauma surrounds bathrooms; dark bathrooms terrified our children.

Among the important first purchases were creative combinations of blinds and curtains. It was vital that light came into the house during the day but also, for the safety of the children, that people could not see into the house during the day or, for the safety of the live-in community, at night. We constantly impressed upon the coworkers the necessity of keeping our lives private and, equally important, not giving the slightest indication that we were watching the street or the neighbor's activity. Shortly before moving in we showed the house to a friend visiting from Australia. He went outside on the street to take a photograph of the house. A man came out of the house across the street and asked brusquely, "What are you doing?" "My friends just bought this house and I am taking a picture," our friend explained. The man replied, "A lot of people around here don't like pictures." Our friend politely asked if he could take it anyway. The man shrugged and went back in his house.

On another day David was working in the house alone. Some of the neighborhood women paid him a visit. They told him they definitely did not want us there. They had heard that the house would be a safe house. They explained that a safe house did not stay secret for long and very soon the abusers would show up. This would make the neighborhood even more violent. "We don't need any more violence around here," they said. David explained in his British accent and Irish ways that the house would primarily serve children who had been homeless. Convinced, they responded in a neighborly way, saying, "We will pass the word."

The day we moved into the house many children assembled on the street to watch. A few adults stood in doorways. Our small van pulled up and we unloaded the simple furnishings from our studio apartment, which included no flat-screen TV and no impressive music system. Some of the children wanted to come in. They saw a sparsely furnished house. We explained that we would be making childcare rooms on the ground floor and that some friends would be coming to share the house and live in the now empty bedrooms. The children inspected the house carefully; finding nothing of interest, they went back out but promised to monitor our progress.

True to their word, at some point every day they peered over the fence while David built a playhouse in the back garden. They wanted to know what it was, why he was building it, how he was building it, and most importantly, if they could play in it. David told them they could when it was finished. The daily question then shifted to, "Is it finished yet?" The day he said yes more than a dozen children immediately streamed into the yard to play.

The front garden had a low wire fence, one flowering bush, and a somewhat daunting amount of weeds. We pulled the weeds, improved the soil, and built a little path with lovely bricks a board member had left over from her landscaping. Another friend had a lavender nursery, enabling us to plant lots and lots of lavender. Near the fence we planted climbing honeysuckle and on the side of the house a small rose garden including a yellow climbing rose that became magnificent, filling the entire side wall of the house. It was important that the first experience children and mothers had when approaching the house was one of calm and beauty.

Later many mothers would speak about the beauty and order of the house and the gardens, commenting that, when they had first arrived, they wondered if they had come to the right address; they said it seemed too clean and cared for to be meant for their children. In the summer we added several profusely flowering bushes and sunflowers, which grew to towering heights, thrilling the children. The Sophia Project children and the neighborhood children truly delighted in what was for them a unique experience, picking a small bouquet of flowers for their mothers. We tried to make sure this was possible most of the year. By the second year there were other small flower gardens in front yards, transforming the formerly scruffy look of the street.

But it was not paradise, as evidenced by the following note, which we wrote to our neighbor after several conversations failed to produce any change:

> Dear Mr. _____,
>
> I am writing to you regarding a significant rat problem that is, as far as I can tell, coming from your property. The area behind the storage unit that is in your driveway seems to be the source. We have seen several rats there and just yesterday during the day two rats ran along the fence. These were both young rats running along the fence in daylight. I would be concerned in any case but as you may know we have very young and very vulnerable children here. Many of them would be unable to cope with a rat bite. Please let me know immediately that you will be dealing with this aggressively this week as it does pose a serious health risk to all of us.

Happily, that cleared it up. Other dangerous, serious problems were much more intractable. The frequent sound of police helicopters low overhead sent everyone, children and adults, scrambling inside out of range of the imminent "police activity." One night shortly after we moved in, the police, in pursuit of two men who had abandoned a stolen car and were now on foot, pounded on the front door and when opened, rushed up the stairs and aimed their rifles at the playhouse, the same playhouse that had during the day given so much joy to the neighborhood children. At night it was not unusual to hear gunshots and sirens.

We carefully limited the time we spent outside in front of the house or in the front garden to only essential activities, such as gardening and normal comings and goings. For the first years the coworkers all lived in one house. During that time we made absolutely sure we kept our private lives inside the house. When we had to walk on the street, as when accompanying children, we did so strictly in our capacity as providers of therapeutic childcare. In this way we kept ourselves safe and established a non-intrusive presence.

We were of course helpful whenever appropriate. For example, some of our neighbors had been petitioning the city for a speed bump on the road to slow down the drug- and gang-related cars racing down the street, often narrowly missing playing children. The city discouraged speed bumps for several reasons, including that they slow down emergency response vehicles. A local woman came to our door with the petition, saying the neighbors wanted a speed bump because "They are going to kill our children." She looked around a bit warily and then continued, "I am a Christian, you are welcome here," inferring that that was not everyone's sentiment. Having a childcare facility on the petition gave it more weight and a speed bump was placed directly in front of Sophia House. This was not all good; while it did deter speeding, drivers who still sped either came to a screeching stop right in front of the house or flew across the bump with a crash. But it was on the whole positive, because it gave us a way to support our neighbors.

Partly because of these efforts we were seen, even in the first year, as a safe place for children. Coming home one afternoon we found our seven-year-old neighbor on the front step. He looked up at us and quietly said, "My mom told me to come over here to be safe." We went next door to see what was happening. No one was home so we returned with the boy to our house. Many hours later he saw his dad walking down the street and ran to him. His dad listened to his son, looked up at us, and gave us a world-weary wave. The boy's mother did not return. Understandably the child did not smile very often. So it was always great to see him beaming when he came over to build elaborate structures with his favorite big pal Paul, one of the coworkers.

Four years after buying Sophia House, we received an astonishingly kind gift: the Omidyar Network Fund paid off our mortgage, which enabled us to buy the building that we soon named Myrtle House.[4] Myrtle House was affordable, large enough, within walking distance to Sophia House, and not occupied by families who would be displaced. In fact, it was a derelict drug house. Individual rooms were padlocked and the house was heated by stove burners turned on high with a fan blowing the warmed air through the kitchen. We replaced the foundation, rewired and re-plumbed the whole house, and completely demolished the interior except for the framing and the stained glass windows in front. We were chosen as a project of Rebuilding Together

Oakland, a nonprofit whose main focus is renovating low-income senior housing. Rebuilding Together helped with some interior renovations and greatly assisted with the landscaping. We planted birch trees and roses in the front; the ample, sunny, side yard had room for a wonderful play space, a big vegetable and herb garden, and three fruit trees.

As the work became more visible to the neighbors one man came up to us and said, "It's really great that you didn't just knock it down, just fixed it up. Yeah, fixed it up! Gives me hope about myself." Other neighbors said it was important for their children to see something that was falling apart and rundown become transformed and made beautiful.

When asked about Sophia Project, the woman living next door to Myrtle House said, "First of all it was a drug house here before Sophia Project came and it was very violent, rowdy, loud, dirty, I was afraid a lot. And once Sophia Project came in everything started to look up. First it impacted me of course. There was a horrible tree in the yard here and as soon as it was cut down it was like I could feel light, get more light in my room, which helped me a lot. And then it seemed like the whole neighborhood, seemed like it lit up after that. It's cleaner and it even smells better. I mean the flowers around here, the natural habitat, the snails and the butterflies and things are appreciated by me because they weren't here before. It seems like our neighbors are being more respectful of just general people walking the streets. Before, you know, they were very rude and disrespectful and now that they see that somebody from another part of a world has come into ours, per se, and is trying to help. And once they see, what I've seen is that the people that see people help, they start helping themselves and helping each other. So it's been a blessing this place being here."

Many people stopped by to ask how they could get help with their house renovations. The Sophia Project coworkers collaborated with Rebuilding Together Oakland to identify seniors in the neighborhood whose houses needed renovations and volunteered on the chosen projects the following year.

A few times a year we had events in which neighbors participated. At our back-to-school event, especially in the early years when there were many young children living in the neighborhood, more than 40 children picked out a backpack, filled it with school supplies from our back-to-school "store" in the back yard, and then helped themselves to refreshments and a little play time. Sometimes we received donations such as canned food in quantities that allowed us to share more widely. On such occasions we put everything we had in the yard, neatly sorted and attractively presented. Neighborhood families took what they needed. People came from the nearby halfway house and senior center. Some Sophia Project mothers took food, diapers, and other supplies to people in great need living nearby but unable to come themselves. In this way we, with the mothers, helped meet the needs of neighbors not in our programs.

After we had two houses, interns and staff often walked the block and a half between Sophia House and Myrtle House. Because they carefully followed the protocol, there were no incidents. One intern who did not follow the guidelines was hassled, but not seriously harmed, when she walked through a group of teenagers drinking on the corner. That was of course terrible for her and additionally it tore a hole in the sheath of safety we had built up. This then needed to be built up again, necessitating even more restraint on the street. Young coworkers at Sophia House would sometimes have private conversation in the garden or, worse, sit in the sun on the front steps. Each time I would hear about it from frustrated people on the street who were trying to help ensure our safety in the neighborhood. The houses were never broken into, although a few things were taken from the yard when inadvertently left out at night.

Attentiveness, mindfulness, consistency, and respectful behavior were essential for our safety and were often returned in kind, as can be seen in this anecdote: Each week for two years, one of the interns picked the street trash out of the plants along our fence. One week the usual group of young men was hanging on the sidewalk; usually they would simply move a little further down the street when the trash was being picked up. This time, as the intern began to collect the trash, one of the young men said, "We'll pick it up," and started putting the trash in a bag. "I'll ask the guys to be more careful," he said. The others nodded in a very hip but definite assent. They kept it relatively clean after that. This was a startling story in our violent neighborhood. The quiet, hard-won, powerful capacity for care had spread.

Again and again we encountered a deep generosity of spirit, allowing us to live safely. A few months after moving into Sophia House I noticed a small statue of Martin Luther King Jr. nestled into a corner of the garden, deeply hidden in the flowers. We didn't know who put it there; months later it was gone. I never knew if we were meant to take it inside or leave it there. Hopefully it is now gracing another place in need.

One day while I was winding honeysuckle through the wire fence a young woman dressed in a business suit stopped to watch. "I didn't know plants could grow on a fence," she said. "Yes, some will climb and cling," I answered. Then looking at her face I quickly saw what she meant. Tracing the vine from the fence to the ground I said, "But they need to start in the ground." She smiled as she understood something new. It was simply a lack of exposure. This was a phenomenon we frequently encountered, a lack of relationship to the natural world, sometimes simply a lack of exposure and other times a result of living in crisis. Fear narrows consciousness. Our mothers and many people in the neighborhood had been living their lives in crisis, as if a big truck was heading right for them. If one imagines this for oneself for a moment, it can quickly be seen that one's consciousness is completely filled with the oncoming truck and what to do to get out of the way. There is no awareness of the surrounding nature or music or art or other human beings. We worked briefly with a high school teacher who taught in a school a few blocks away. She told us she had classes of high school students who had never been to San Francisco, twenty minutes away on public transportation, and likely had not been out of West Oakland.

Neighborhood Children

The gardens were an important point of contact, although sometimes not in ways we would have chosen. While sitting downstairs with a few neighbor children ages 3 to 12, the mail arrived with the biodynamic preparations for the garden. The children watched as I opened small plastic packets of while silica and larger packets of green and brown barrel compost. They nodded knowingly. "No," I said, "They are not drugs, they are medicines for the garden." They smiled; even the very young children were skeptical. There was no choice but to immediately mix the preparations and with help from the children apply them to the garden, regardless of the fact that all the plants were not yet in and we had planned to apply the silica later. Thus the children were convinced the preparations were not drugs as even we were unlikely to waste them in that way. This did, however, offer further evidence of our strange ways, which now included giving medicine to the soil and plants.

When appropriate, we gave odd jobs to older children. One twelve-year-old boy in particular often came over to earn money. He was in kin foster care, living diagonally across the street in a very crowded apartment. We tried to teach him to mow the driveway and other simple chores. He proved to be quite impervious to instruction, preferring to come by the house with a seemingly endless stream of boxes filled neatly with assortments of chocolate that needed to be sold to buy uniforms for an impressive number of teams he played on. This was surprising for a boy who seemed to rarely actually attend school, although he knew better than to come over anytime he was supposed to be in school. Still, better chocolates than other things; we were good customers. After two years he moved away but we saw him once downtown when he was about 20. He came over to us smiling that same charming smile. "Do you remember me?" he asked. "Of course D, we will always remember you," we answered. He stopped for a moment, with a warm but serious smile he waved, "Ok, thanks."

The neighbor children came as often as we could manage to supervise them. Even the older children liked to play with the toys. In addition to free play we worked with the children on drawing, painting, crafts, doll-making, puppet shows, and finger knitting. Snack time was a favorite. One afternoon as we were driving away, a little girl came from across the street to the gate. "When you come home can we do that thing when everyone sits at the table real quiet and sings and we all get a cup and napkin?" That "thing" is snack time. Her little face so hopeful, it is so little to ask. I will always be deeply grateful for the opportunity to say yes.

Once we started the licensed childcare programs, the neighbor children understood that they could not drop by if the childcare was open, unless they were enrolled in the program. We reserved one or two spots in the program for neighborhood children who did not technically qualify but whose families were struggling economically. After a few years the man and woman across the street—the same man who had brusquely questioned our friend photographing our house—had a baby girl and joined the infant program at Myrtle House. The neighbors next door to Myrtle House also joined the infant program. And of course from the beginning several Sophia Project families lived in the neighborhood and walked to Sophia House each day.

The First Year

Outside

Our children had spent very little time outdoors. Understandably they were at first wary about nature and being outside in general. Their neighborhoods were not safe for outside play; there literally was nowhere to play. If there happened to be a nearby public park, it was likely taken over by drug deals and littered with needles and condoms. Even at Sophia House it was not safe to play in front. The children did not spend time there unless they were picking flowers, accompanied by an adult. Building a high fence and gate around the back yard where the children would play was a priority, as was making it beautiful. We did everything we could to nurture our children's relationship to nature and the outdoors, and they grew to love it.

In addition to the playhouse, we added a heavy-duty swing and built a big sandbox. We made a small hill at one end of the yard, very important for all sorts of games and for simply running up and down and resting at the top. At the time, our volunteers were not sure about the sanity of making a hill but, if they could have seen the years of wonderful play it afforded, they would have been thrilled. We kept the middle section of the yard clear and planted it with grass, replanting it every year.

To accommodate the neighbor's thorny and roaming bougainvillea we built a trellis overhead spanning six feet from the fence to the side of the house. During its long blooming season, it created a house made of bright pink flowers. Another neighbor's house had an old nut tree that still produced enough nuts to attract the squirrels that were used to having undisputed reign in our formerly abandoned yard. Sometimes they buried their nuts in the sand box and then chattered noisily when the children gleefully found them. There was also an old plum tree whose remaining three branches were good for climbing and still produced small, sweet plums. We planted three apple trees near the new playhouse. Accompanying the trees from bare, to leaf, to blossom, and to fruit was a nourishing experience for the children and one in which they took great interest and pleasure, especially when the cycle repeated.

Although the back yard had only morning sun, we planted the small vegetable patch there because it kept the children safe from the eyes of strangers and unwanted contact. The children were initially horrified that we would eat things from the ground. They patiently and repeatedly explained that just as it was not OK to get your clothes dirty, it was definitely not OK to eat from the ground. In time they delighted in the growth and changes they saw in the plants. Although we needed to supplement our harvest, we tried to grow what they would eat at lunch: peas, broccoli, beans, potatoes, carrots, and a pumpkin for Halloween. I say "a" pumpkin because one is all we ever had; but it was much loved. These small miracles of fruiting trees, squirrel's nuts, a pumpkin, space to run, things to climb, and safety brought joy and true healing—for all of us.

The Childcare Rooms

When entering the classroom the first thing many adults saw was the large mural (beautifully painted by Sharry Wright). The painted scene, familiar to many, depicted children crossing a bridge guided and guarded from behind by an angel. In our depiction, the bridge was made of the same material as the actual floor next to the mural, suggesting that the bridge ended in the classroom. The children depicted were of different ethnicities; the angel was of an indeterminate ethnicity, silver hair, warm skin tones, perhaps Native American or Polynesian. Additionally the mural contained images of the four elements—water, earth, air, and fire—all the kingdoms of nature, as well as the sky and the sun.

Our mothers did not make a distinction between religion and spirituality. In a single conversation it was difficult to explain this difference and the principles underlying the education. In any case they were in survival mode and would be unlikely to refuse to bring their child on religious grounds. In view of this situation, it was important to be clear about our view of the human being. The mural served to inform the mothers that at Sophia Project, spirit, the human being, and the whole of nature were recognized and valued.

Because many Sophia Project mothers objected, especially for their sons, to the pink playrooms at Raphael House (the San Francisco shelter where many Sophia Project families had lived), we painted the rooms in warm peach colors using the lazure technique. In most other respects the rooms were set up in ways similar to a traditional Waldorf kindergarten, including rainbow cloths serving as roofs for playhouses, a nature table, house building materials, handmade cloth dolls of many ethnicities, shells, stones, logs, colored cloths, standing puppets, wooden animals, beeswax crayons, and musical instruments.

There were also some important modifications. We had many more books than are usually found in a Waldorf classroom. Our children were at very high risk for illiteracy. Some parents could not read at all, many others were not fluent readers. Their homes usually did not contain books and the children rarely witnessed people reading or writing. For this reason, in addition to telling stories at puppet shows and story time, we read aloud to the children. Carefully chosen multicultural books were always available in the classroom. Eventually most children chose to look at books for some part of each day. Hearing books read aloud and acquiring an appreciation of books and stories are critical early literacy skills.

For those children just beginning to attend Sophia Project we included toys with which they were familiar. Toys such as traditional puzzles, blocks, and lacing frames offer more structure than the classic Waldorf toys, which are intentionally open-ended and encourage imaginative play. We gradually put the more structured toys away during the morning Waldorf kindergarten time.

In their first few weeks, children would perhaps be unable to imagine, for example, the blue silk cloth as water. Faced with this situation it might be necessary for the teacher to quietly say, "This is the water." After several weeks in the kindergarten this prompting was no longer necessary. The young children soon entered enthusiastically into a world of story, play, imagination, and simple artistic activity.

We found that children from the population we served often required protected playtime and some initial guidance in building their imagination "muscle." While I was working at Raphael House, an Emergency Room nurse from San Francisco General Hospital sought me out. At that time, , the emergency room was one of the few places a low-income family could receive medical care for non-emergency illness, such as a fever. If one person in a family became sick, a mother would take the whole family to the emergency room because there was no one else to watch the children. Consequently the ER waiting area was often loud and chaotic.

Over time the ER staff noticed that some children were able to entertain themselves quietly. These children often had some colored cloths with which they wove stories. Grateful for the quiet, the staff began to ask about these "magic" cloths. After speaking to many of the mothers, it gradually became clear that the children had all spent time at Raphael House where they had received their cloths. The nurse had come to inquire about obtaining these cloths for the ER waiting area.

I explained that after several months in the Raphael House children's programs, many young children had acquired the capacity to play imaginatively. At the end of their stay they were often given a set of play cloths to take with them. The ER staff had witnessed this imaginative play and were hoping that other children, when supplied with the cloths, would also quietly be absorbed in play. Naturally I gave the nurse a set of cloths, but cautioned that without the inner unseen activity of imagination the cloths themselves would not be magic. She took them anyway and later affirmed that without the child's inner activity, the cloths became mere rags.

Some traditional Waldorf toys were not used at Sophia Project, notably gnomes and fleece pictures. Gnomes were viewed with suspicion by our African-American families, particularly winter gnomes dressed all in white with white pointed hoods. We simply did not use them and we sewed down the points of any other hooded dolls or figures.

The children who were afraid of the fleece pictures insisted that the pictures be covered up at naptime. We tried making them in front of the children, when this still did not appease them we took them away. It seemed the pictures were too airy; the children perceived them as ghost-like.

Food

Many of our children came from homes where food was scarce. Often children arrived in the morning without having had dinner the night before. Everything to do with food was important: including growing and preparing, eating meals and snacks, and taking food home from the Sophia House pantry.

Every day we served a warm breakfast, a cooked lunch, and three substantial snacks. Lunch was the main meal of the day for the whole community. We developed a nutritious, child-friendly menu that repeated every two weeks. Many a child's first question upon arriving in the morning was, "What's for lunch today?" The school-aged children could joyfully list the menu for the week while the younger children, upon hearing the main dish, could enthusiastically list the side dishes for that meal. The ability to confidently predict the schedule and future events of each day is a necessary component in healing trauma.

Predictable, peaceful meals and snacks were essential for engaged play, circle, and story time. Knowing they would have enough to eat enabled the children to relax and to realize that it was not necessary to wait near the kitchen to secure a place in line for food. It took time to become used to the practice of washing hands, sitting at a set table, singing grace, and then being served a plate of food. It was most difficult for the first small group of children. As other children joined, those already familiar with the program would assure the new children that there was plenty of food and that washing hands was an essential part of the process, not a ploy to distract them while the others gobbled up the food.

The children were much more comfortable with recognizable packaged or fast foods. To ensure they would eat this new kind of food it was important to be consistent in both type and presentation of the food offered. For example, yogurt was offered as a part of breakfast, a single kind at a time with one kind of fruit. We were eager for the children to eat the yogurt as an antidote to their many stomach and digestive problems. Slowly they began to do so until one morning a thrift-minded coworker mixed all the remaining kinds of yogurt together. Not only did the children not eat the yogurt that day, it took three weeks before they would try it again, or indeed any unfamiliar food.

Poor nutrition also contributed to the children's weak immune systems; we steadily incorporated more nutritious food into their diets. In the beginning it was difficult to coax the children to eat fresh vegetables and fruits. Growing and harvesting some of them, even in very small quantities, was pivotal to the process. Stories and songs that were in any way associated with the food we ate also helped entice the children to try unfamiliar food while still meeting individual dietary needs. Equally important was time in the kitchen helping to prepare snacks and meals; having a turn as "lunch helper" was highly prized.

The children relished taking home items they had cooked or baked. Baking with Christl Bender was especially cherished. Twice a year Christl, an older Camphiller, came to visit for several weeks. During that time she would bake bread with every child, absorbing each one in the wonderful imagery of the process of bread coming to life. Every child would make one loaf for the community and proudly take the other beautifully braided loaf home, where it was truly valued and appreciated. The now grown children still speak about and cherish the memory of this experience.

Clothing

Once I was showing some colleagues photos of the kindergarten I had started in South Africa at Camphill Hermanus. Looking at the children's clothes, one usually very warm-hearted colleague criticized the lack of dress code. It was true; most of the children wore ill-fitting clothes, many with logos. It is easy to forget that different environments generate different circumstances. The children from the township had very few clothes; they regularly came in the same clothes, washed and pressed each night. Shoes were expensive and, in many families, shared. There was of course no thought of requiring a certain kind of clothing.

Although the situation, in Sophia Project was less extreme than South Africa, clothing nevertheless was a challenge. A washer and dryer in the childcare space were indispensable for the daily loads of children's clothes as well as for use by some of the mothers at particular junctures on the journey from homelessness to stability. It is expensive and difficult to travel by bus with bags of laundry to a laundromat in a safe area. Additionally, if their children's clothes were frequently dirty from a day's play, these mothers would be seen by many social workers and other professionals, not as a mother who valued their children's vigorous play, but rather as a mother unable to care properly for her children. Such an assessment could have dire repercussions.

Naturally we fully encouraged play. We had many extra sets of clothes so that we could change the children when they were wet or dirty. We made sure that at the end of each day every child was in clean clothes with combed hair and clean hands and face.

As in South Africa, shoes needed special protection. Upon arrival the children carefully put their shoes in their cubbies and changed into the slippers we provided for inside play. We outfitted each child with boots, raincoats, warm jackets, hats, outside shoes, and coveralls or other weather-appropriate clothing for outside play. Except for the hats, these were all uniform in style and color and so able to be changed around to fit different children each year. Far from objecting, the children delighted in having the same jackets.

Each child received a sheet and small pillow for naptime, along with a quilt, lovingly made by hand for each child. The children took their quilts with them when they left the daily programs. Myrtle House supplies also included diapers and other toddler- and baby-specific items.

Boots, shoes, coats, extra clothes, blankets and sheets were all kept in four-foot open cubbies that accommodated all of this and still allowed space for a small child to sit atop the bottom shelf. On their first day at Sophia House, children chose a cubby adorned with a hand-drawn peaceful image; this remained their cubby as long as they were in the daily program. This ordered, pleasant space was precious to the children.

For many, their cubby was the only space that was truly theirs alone; they simply enjoyed sitting in it, playing with some small toy. For others it was a place of refuge where they found comfort and safety in the snug space.

Sleep

Many children did not sleep well at home, often arriving in the morning exhausted. They were troubled by nightmares and described seeing bad spirits of various kinds when they were falling asleep. Violence in their buildings and neighborhoods produced stress and fear. Although we helped the mothers create healthy bedtime rhythms, they were often too exhausted themselves to transform the atmosphere around their child.

Most children slept soundly at Sophia House. After lunch the main playroom was turned into a nap room. Shelves of toys were covered with soft colored cloths and nap cots with sheets and quilts were set out in the same pattern each day. Every coworker was needed at naptime to settle a small group of two or three children. Each child chose a book and a doll or toy. The coworker read the book and gently rubbed the child's back as she fell asleep to singing or lyre music. The coworker would then go to their next child and repeat the process.

First Coworkers

Each child's success depended on skilled and experienced coworkers. Under our agreement with Raphael House family shelter, David spent every weekday morning in San Francisco managing Raphael House operations, and I was there afternoons and evenings directing children's services. We were immensely fortunate to be joined at Sophia Project by two experienced coworkers, Silene Gemmrick and Eric Beumer, with whom I had worked at the Camphill Hermanus School in South Africa some five years earlier.

After his time in South Africa, Eric, an experienced housefather and curative education teacher, had rejoined Camphill Orion in the Netherlands. Camphill Orion fully sponsored Eric for five months to assist in founding Sophia Project. Silene, a Waldorf high school graduate, was just eighteen years old when she assisted me in starting a multiracial kindergarten within Camphill Hermanus. After South Africa she returned to Germany. Two years later she came to Raphael House for several months to work with me in creating Waldorf-based art programs. By the time Sophia Project started Silene had earned an anthroposophical art therapy degree. She joined us for the grueling first year.

Having worked together before, it was easy for us to communicate both necessary information and profound questions and ideas. We sat together most evenings to look at the work. My colleagues had their own inner practice and worked out of the anthroposphical view of the human being. They were experienced in working with vulnerable children, were practiced in working out of Steiner's child development principles, and were capable community builders. When they left, we needed to create a training that addressed all these aspects of the work and was suitable for young and inexperienced people, including some with no exposure to Steiner's work. We were joined by Anna Sands (now Anna Pope), a Camphill staff child needing one year of supervised student teaching to complete her Waldorf Early Years/Kindergarten teacher certificate, and several young people wishing to serve as interns for varying lengths of time.

Endnotes

1. Among her many other gifts, board member Kathy Gower faithfully cooked lunch for the entire community of children, adults, and coworkers once a week, every week for eleven years.

2. Elizabeth Roberts and Elias Amidon, eds., *Life Verses* (New York: Harper Collins Publishers, 1996), p 13.

3. The third-floor renovation was made possible largely through a generous donation by Seymour Kaufman. This was a gift of faith. Sy had just met us, Sophia Project work with the children had not yet begun, and he was unfamiliar with Camphill or Waldorf education. Later Sy became a board member and continued to be a faithful friend to Sophia Project.

4. Iqbal and Janet Paroo, the force behind this gift, continued to be great friends to Sophia Project, providing generous support and expert assistance in many areas. Janet also served on our board of trustees.

Chapter Two:
Coworker Education

Initially, almost all coworkers joined Sophia Project as one-year interns. Most were Waldorf school graduates or had grown up in Camphill or other anthroposophical communities. Many, however, came to Sophia Project through the Americorps program and did not have a Waldorf background (Sophia Project was part of the Camphill Americorps program, administered at that time by the Camphill Coworker Development Office in Hudson, New York). Because the interns lacked professional experience, David and I needed to develop an intern program that would focus primarily on the needs of the children and mothers, while also supporting the interns and enabling them to serve effectively. Julia Wolfson, our friend and experienced Camphill consultant, helped to create the first intern documents, which outlined the program and put in place important practices such as exit interviews. Exit interviews, always conducted by someone other than ourselves, were reviewed by David and me at the end of each year in order to update the description of the conditions, experiences, and responsibilities that incoming interns could expect.

By 2003 we had developed a twelve-page document entitled *Sophia Project Agreement for an Internship in Service* (reproduced in Part Two of this volume). This description of coworker life made clear the need for stamina and inner resourcefulness as well as balanced emotional and mental health. The agreement also described support for interns, including in-service training, monthly outside processing/counseling[1], room and board, medical insurance, a modest stipend, assistance with student loan payments, and return travel money.

After the first two years of operation, coworkers began to commit to a second or third year of service. For some interns, working at Sophia Project satisfied requirements for Waldorf early childhood teaching certificates or clinical psychology practicum hours. By 2009 we had a dedicated and skilled group of coworkers, each of whom had worked at Sophia Project for at least three years.

The most significant growth in coworker stability was the up-front three-year commitment made by Martin Alfred and Jana Pazourkova (now Jana Alfred) in 2006. Martin grew up as a staff child in Camphill School Scotland. After serving for a time in the early years of Sophia Project, he returned at our request. Jana had been a coworker at Camphill School Scotland, where she obtained her BA in curative education. Martin and Jana's skill and dedication gave us confidence and a solid base for deepening and expanding the work.

Sophia Project was founded as a conscious expression of a wider approach to curative education and the Camphill community impulse. We were encouraged by the following excerpt from Karl König's "A Camphill Letter":

> A so-called welfare society which starts to forget human values—a human race which denies racial problems and has invented at the same time means of mass destruction that can kill millions in a few minutes—a social order which forgot the divine order and searches for new ethics that can't be found any more because of the loss of belief in God—this generates a new array of tasks: to help the frail, disabled, lame and sick persons, and those who have become defenceless and depressive to gain once more their human dignity. Is it not a great miracle? Mankind on the brink of self-destruction creates something new that grows like a new seed within a sinking society. A holistic curative education resembles the developing seed in a rotting fruit. We only need to understand the idea of curative education in its widest sense, then we will be able to perceive its true mission . . . it has the potential to become a worldwide force that can meet the "threat to the individual" that now prevails. The "curative educational approach" should express itself in every field of social work, in spiritual welfare, in the care for the elderly, in the rehabilitation of the mental patients as well as the disabled, in the guidance of orphans and refugees, of suicide candidates and the desperate; but also in development aid, in the international peace corps and similar attempts. If we truly still want to consider ourselves to be human, then this is the only possible answer we can give today while mankind dances close to the abyss . . .

> Only the help from person to person—the encounter of ego to ego, the realization of the other person's individuality without judging his confession, beliefs, world view and political education—simply the direct and one to one encounter of two personalities—is able to create this kind of curative education that is able to meet the threat to the

inner human being in a healing manner. However, this will only be possible on the basis of a thorough and heart-felt wisdom.[2]

Coworker education at Sophia Project consisted of several components:
1. A comprehensive in-service program in which all live-in coworkers fully participated
2. Supervision every two weeks.
3. Individual endeavors including completion of education requirements such as supervised student teaching or clinical psychology hours.
4. Participation of some coworkers in the BA in curative education degree offered through the Curative Education Program at Camphill Special Schools, Glenmoore PA (now a part of the Camphill Academy).

Sophia Project was a satellite site for the first two years of the Camphill BA program. The wider Sophia Project community taught the required courses or, in alignment with the requirements of the Curative Education Program, designed courses to meet the special needs of children from the population Sophia Project served. It was an honor as well as a significant undertaking to be the first satellite location.

~

The Camphill Impulse
Sophia Project Newsletter, 2013

During my time at Sophia Project I always appreciated its connection to the Camphill movement through being an affiliate of Camphill North America. I found it especially inspiring that Sophia Project was unique in its manifestation of the Camphill impulse. The Camphill movement, which began in Scotland in 1942, has a mission to support vulnerable people in need of care, no matter what their background, through creating life-sharing communities where mutual caring and learning takes place. I found Sophia Project's dedication to community, and its acting out of love, inspiring as it is so difficult to maintain yet it is so healing for the families that are supported by it. While at Sophia Project I was fortunate to be able to study at the Sophia Project satellite of the Camphill School of Curative Education and Social Therapy. I have now graduated from my studies and I am working in Camphill in Scotland.

Martin Alfred, former coworker

~

In-Service Education, Orientation:

Every summer, after finding appropriate care for anyone needing it, Sophia Project closed for three weeks. Just prior to reopening, every member of the live-in community fully participated in an intensive six-day orientation retreat that enabled us to cohere as a group for the year ahead. The orientation included discussions regarding the mission of Sophia Project and its relationship to Camphill, Waldorf education, and Raphael House. Experienced Sophia Project coworkers shared important information concerning neighborhood safety, finances, the healing conditions created by the live-in community, guiding principles, working with the children and mothers, the distinct purpose and form of weekly meetings, and the programs. These topics and others were developed in more detail in meetings through the year. We also spent time together in artistic activity, outings, cooking meals, and sharing our life stories.

It was understood that we were to live simply, so that our resources, both inner and outer, were directed to the needs of the children and mothers. We were always tightly staffed and could not financially support extra coworkers. During orientation everyone received transparent, detailed financial information, including project-wide and coworker-specific budgets as well as information regarding fundraising, the role of the board of trustees, and the role of volunteers.

The orientation week's activities highlighted the importance of the live-in community serving as the vessel for the programs. Our mindful life together created the healing conditions necessary for transformation of the children, the mothers, and ourselves. Throughout the year we regularly focused on practices that supported the health of each individual's inner life and the health of our shared social life.

The biographies of the children were treated respectfully; details of the mothers' lives were confidential. New coworkers often underestimated the thoughtful, deep, and gentle quality of work that was required to guide the children effectively. In order to respond appropriately in their first days, new interns needed to understand some of the children's specific circumstances. After hearing descriptions of the children's biographies and situations, we built up, as a group, a list of feelings, conditions, struggles, hardships, and obstacles the children were experiencing. This list included fear, chaos, homelessness, fragmentation, the strain of unknown and unpredictable life circumstances, uncertainty, feelings of insignificance and not belonging, malnourishment, harsh and unclean environments, wounded relationships, lack of experiences of the natural world, abuse, violence, and developmental delays. Next to each of these we then explored, as a starting point, qualities that could bring healing. In this way new coworkers could begin to understand not only the difficulties the children faced daily, but also the warmth and thoughtful attentiveness required for genuine healing. Here is a typical list of difficult experiences and possible responses:

fear . . . . love and safety

chaos. . . . . order

homelessness. . . . . sustained relationship

fragmentation . . . . wholeness

unpredictable lives. . . . . consistency

uncertainty. . . . . predictable rhythm

not important . . . . important, each one every time

not belonging. . . . . belonging, community

malnourished . . . . nourishing food

abuse. . . . . gentleness

violence. . . . . nonviolence

harsh, unclean environments. . . . . beauty and cleanliness

wounded personal relationships . . . . healthy relationships

lack of relationship to the world . . . . experience that forms relationships

developmental delays . . . . appropriate curriculum

Through continuous in-service education, coworkers would gain greater clarity about the insights and practices through which community life and Waldorf early childhood education could bring these essential healing qualities. As a foundation for this study, during orientation we briefly introduced aspects of the anthroposophical view of the human being.

Especially for the mothers, dignity can begin to be regained through the coworkers' recognition of the depth, height, and breadth of every human being through time. During orientation we pictured the human being with feet on the earth and head in the cosmos. We conveyed an image of great breadth, coming from the spirit through many incarnations—here now in this incarnation, and continuing into the future. The image of the human being, held in its wholeness by the live-in community, created a restorative environment.

Similarly, when contemplating a child, coworkers were encouraged to visualize, next to the wounded child, a healthy child with an intact spirit. This visualization helped coworkers see each child's strengths, and point to the particular quality that, as teachers, we would need to find within ourselves to support each child's transition from wounded to healthy.

Orientation fostered the understanding that many of our children lived face-to-face with powerful, specific evils—injustice, violence, and addiction. In the future our children would be in a position to transform these evils. To do so, they would need capacities and skills for transformation without which they could well be drawn into the fire that threatens us all.

Transformation at Sophia Project took place one day at a time, with patience and insight, by single gestures, by gentle words, by moments of joy, playfulness, and comforting silence.

Sophia Project Newsletter, 2002

When one of our four-year-old boys first came to Sophia House he was a whirlwind of fists, hitting other children many times a day. He has experienced much violence in his short life. Now a whole week can go by without even so much as a push. His face is calm, no longer hard and tight. Still, he will need some time to make this newfound way of being his own. One day, while playing with the ducks in the water, he looked up and quietly said, "I'm a good boy now." "Yes, you are a good boy." We meet in a smile, it has been a long journey; he goes back to his play, singing softly to himself.

A successful beginning of the year also relied upon a basic understanding of three additional components:

1. The importance of sustained relationship.
2. The significance of maintaining conditions for daily unfolding of normal, healthy child development while also attending to wounds stemming from trauma.
3. The necessity of every coworker's inner work in creating conditions for transformation.

It is broadly accepted that a safe, stable environment and ongoing nurturing relationships are crucial components of the young child's well-being. The Centers for Disease Control and Prevention considers these components central to healthy development. Further, nurturing, sustained relationship is central to the development of resilience. The Center on the Developing Child at Harvard University states:

> Reducing the effects of significant adversity on children's healthy development is essential to the progress and prosperity of any society. Science tells us that some children develop resilience, or the ability to overcome serious hardship, while others do not. Understanding why some children do well despite adverse early experiences is crucial, because it can inform more effective policies and programs that help more children reach their full potential. . . . The single most common factor for children who develop resilience is at least one stable and committed relationship with a supportive parent, caregiver, or other adult.[2]

In the fragmented, chaotic world of homelessness, children are frequently cared for by a young, highly stressed mother and a succession of relative strangers. The lack of stability adversely affects their cognitive, emotional, and social development. It was crucial that the programs at Sophia Project be stable and predictable. This was initially difficult for some interns to grasp. They were eager to bring their own abilities to the program and sometimes found the adherence to routine burdensome. It was difficult for them to understand, for example, that the table needed to always be set in the same way, not because there was something sacred about the placement of the cutlery, but because the unchanged table setting served as a steadying force in the children's chaotic world. During orientation we made it very clear that the children needed the interns as well as the more experienced coworkers to bring the healing qualities of security and continuity. Our community provided stability through a predictable environment anchored by sustained, nurturing relationships with long-term coworkers. Within these established rhythms, interns were able to bring their youthful energy, playfulness, and, in time, appropriate ways to express their ideals and compassion.

The following story of the relationship David and I developed with Cherie is one of many that helped the interns understand the importance of sustained relationship.

Cherie was eleven months old when she and her mother first came to Raphael House shelter during which time I worked with her mother on parenting. As Cherie was nearly three years old when they returned for their second stay, she joined the Raphael House daycare. During this second stay, her mother lost custody of her and Cherie was placed in foster care. This first foster care parent continued Cherie's participation in the Raphael House daycare. There was no charge for the program and Cherie was very attached to the small group of children and to me.

After several months Cherie was moved to what was intended to be a more long-term placement. As these foster parents were willing for Cherie to continue in the program but were unwilling to drive her, David drove every morning to pick her up and took her back each evening. At this point Cherie began writing me "notes," though of course she could not really write. She now spoke very infrequently; she scribbled on pieces of paper and handed them to me. Her foster home was safe but the foster parents did not demonstrate warmth toward Cherie. Each morning Cherie arrived with a note she had written the night before.

Cherie was then transferred to another foster home. These foster parents reacted with hostility to the idea of Cherie continuing at the Raphael House daycare. They would not allow me to contact her or respond to her need to have some contact with me. After some weeks I grew more and more uneasy with the situation. As I did not have any legal standing in her life, it took several attempts to persuade the authorities to make a house visit. When they did they found her in a very sad state. She had essentially been kept in a large box. Tightly held in both little fists were crumpled pieces of paper, her notes to me.

Cherie was then put in another foster home with wonderful people who brought her every day to the daycare and welcomed her involvement with our activities. Throughout grade school and high school she came regularly to Sophia House for respite care. When Cherie entered college in 2014 she lived with us for a semester while we worked out housing and tuition. She is now in her senior year at California State University, a business major with a 3.5 GPA and planning to begin her MBA next year. We see her often. A kind and thoughtful young woman, she enjoys artistic work and hopes to travel the world.

Fostering a calm, regular, nourishing environment was integral to the mothers' and children's healing. At the same time it was vital to respond to the trauma they had experienced. As coworkers we continually attended to both. Sometimes the situation was pictured as encompassing a skillful urgent care trauma center within a beautiful, rhythmically working homestead.

It was crucial that coworkers be inwardly active, engaged in ennobling daily life, deepening their relationships to the world, and learning new skills. In this way we not only modeled ways of being but also joined our children and families in creating an enriched inner and outer life to replace the inner and outer poverty that was a daily challenge for our families.

In-Service Education through the School Year

> If we use Imaginations, we can teach children anything. When they ask what life after death is like, you can show them a pupa of a butterfly and tell them that a soul leaving its body is like a butterfly leaving its pupa, only we cannot see the soul. But your teaching will be convincing only if you yourself believe it when you say that the emergence of a butterfly exemplifies on a lower level what happens with the soul on a higher level. When images become alive in our hearts as a result of reimmersing ourselves in an understanding of the spiritual world through spiritual science, our teaching will be transformed, and we will no longer give children dry, rational truths that coarsen their psyche. We must not use grotesque or comical images, however. We must acknowledge the crucial importance of what underlies these images.
>
> From Rudolf Steiner, *The Secret Stream: Christian Rosenkreuz and Rosicrucianism*[3]

The work with the children and mothers required every coworker's dedicated effort. Each had to focus on his or her own part while maintaining a sense of the whole. After orientation, in-service education was continued through weekly program, teacher, and study meetings, augmented by biweekly individual supervision, biweekly house meetings, and occasional weekend intensives.

All coworkers who had direct contact with the children and mothers attended the weekly program meeting. This core meeting began with a 45-minute study or presentation. Topics included literacy, domestic violence, restraining orders, trauma, nonviolence and compassionate speech, gun violence, white privilege, Waldorf early childhood classroom and curriculum, imitation, fantasy and imagination, rhythm, the kingdoms of nature, artistic work for young children, the significance of individual children's art, child development, sleep, the senses and nutrition. In addition, Sophia Project child study included observation of the child's physical nature, movement, speech, balance, social relationships, artistic work, play, thinking, memory, and careful consideration of the child's biography. The second half of the meeting included informative announcements, follow-up reports, concerns regarding the children, action plans, and matters arising.

Weekend intensives allowed for a deeper focus on children and families. Near the beginning and the middle of each term, we identified:

- Our wishes for each child.
- Next steps, goals and objectives for each child.
- Teacher, program, family, and community support the child would need to accomplish these steps.
- Methods for progress evaluation.
- Methods for recording and review of progress.

For each family we identified:

- The strengths of the family.
- Challenges the family faced.
- Current and most pressing needs.
- An action plan to meet those needs.
- A follow-up timeline.
- A method and timeline for evaluation.

There were always at least two early childhood Waldorf teachers and usually a curative educator among the coworkers. The teachers met every week. Other experienced, anthroposophically trained coworkers also took part in this meeting, which was dedicated to cultivating a deeper understanding of Waldorf early childhood pedagogy, curative education, trauma, and meeting the needs of traumatized children. We frequently studied the twelve senses as described by Rudolf Steiner, and the impact of the disturbance of the lower senses in our young children, especially the sense of life. We strove for clarity regarding the effects of trauma on the physical, emotional, and cognitive development of each child. We focused on curriculum and child development, inner work, and attentive practice in order to develop the ability to understand each child and create the conditions for healing.

The rich weekly study, attended by all live-in coworkers, was devoted to topics other than those directly pertaining to the children and mothers. We studied the core elements of the meditative path described in Rudolf Steiner's foundational book, *How to Know Higher Worlds* (see "Texts Used in Coworker Education" in Part Two of this volume). We also explored other contemplative paths and practices. Coworkers took turns leading studies of anthroposophical ideas, sharing specific expertise, and leading discussions on the civil right movement, non-violence and the life and ideas of Gandhi, Martin Luther King, Jr., and Thomas Merton. We also took up biography work in many forms. Additionally, we were fortunate to have visits from many talented people who led studies and artistic activities.

Practices such as reading for the dead took place in private, but were open to anyone who wished to join. The long-term coworkers, as well as any interns who so wished, agreed to strive to live up to the Sophia Project leading thought:

> Out of love for the children, children who together with their
> mothers have experienced inner and outer poverty, violence, abuse,
> homelessness and a lack of human dignity, we strive to live and work
> together in such a way that our community striving in service of Christ
> is manifest in ways the children can imitate and in which the mothers
> can participate and in so doing can develop the inner capacities needed
> to transform themselves and the world around them, serve the good,
> and gain evermore strength and courage to transform that which robs
> and degrades human dignity.

On weeknights (Monday through Thursday), coworkers ate dinner together. Dinner times were an opportunity to be together socially. On non-respite weekends, coworkers made individual plans. At bi-weekly house meetings we met as individuals, leaving our roles aside, to share and discuss issues arising from living together. We shared housekeeping duties and meal preparation. Each of us had an area of the garden that we tended for a year, often with the support of a biodynamic gardener whose insights and explanations added pleasure to this work.

On Sunday evenings we met to share, in a simple way, the weekly Camphill Bible reading. Coworkers took turns preparing some thoughts on the reading. This practice gave us the opportunity to link with the wider Camphill Community as well as to come together again before starting a new week.

~

Coworker Reflections
Sophia Project newsletter, 2013

It's hard to measure the multiple ways in which the Sophia Project has impacted my life. I can say that when I heard about the project I was 15 years old, this was around 12 years ago. I was inspired by the amazing work that was happening in West Oakland and I became determined to be a part of it. It was a few years later when I was lucky enough to get that opportunity. With full confidence I say that in entering into the work of helping families turn their lives around I was also able to turn my own life around—both spiritually and practically. Working from the impulse of love and kindness allowed a space for caring that the children and families thrived on. Seeing the progress that they made when faced with the most challenging of circumstances gave us all the strength needed to continue. This cycle of respect and compassion led to the creation of one of the most genuine of supportive spaces. My time at the project coupled with updates of the families' continued progress has instilled in me a need to carry the ideals of the project into my current training as a third-year medical student. I believe my patients benefit everyday as a direct result of the skills and mindfulness that I started to develop during my time in West Oakland. For this gift I will always be thankful to the children, families, co-workers and supporters of the Sophia Project.

Jasmin Bradley, former coworker
Jasmin is now a physician beginning her practice in Ohio.

Sophia Project Newsletter, 2013

What kind of influence has Sophia Project had on my life? Profound. Life changing. Everlasting. It was during those years that I found my purpose. I am forever awe-struck when I think about the transformation that I witnessed in our children and families. We provided them a safe space, nurturing relationships, and therapeutic experiences, and they in turn worked tirelessly to heal their wounds, rediscover their light, and become forces of change in their communities.

Jenny Ventura, former coworker
Jen has now completed a master's degree in social welfare
and is working in a children's mental health organization.

Endnotes

1. Professional counseling support for interns was generously made possible by Karen Apana, PhD., Waldorf high school counselor, therapist, artist, and friend to the Sophia Project.

2. Karl Koenig, "Leading Thoughts." *Karl Koenig Archive*, from "Camphill Letter," Föhrenbühl and Saint Prex, 1965. www.karl-koenig-archive.net/mission.htm.

3. Center on the Developing Child, "Resilience" (2015). developingchild.harvard.edu/science/key-concepts/resilience/.

Chapter Three:
Programs

Sophia Project was a direct-service, community-based care and education center for children and families at risk of recurring homelessness. We worked with children and families facing major challenges, but the mothers had (in most cases) moved out of homelessness, made some efforts to stabilize their families, and expressed a clear commitment to work with Sophia Project to create more stability and opportunity for their children.

Our primary goal was to alleviate and if possible reverse the developmental delays and extreme emotional fragility of children who had suffered the traumatic effects of deep poverty, violence, and homelessness. We strove to ensure that the children we served were nurtured, and that their physical, emotional, developmental, educational, and social needs were met while their mothers received time, guidance, and support to acquire new abilities to meet their children's needs and stabilize their families. We did this through therapeutic childcare and an early-childhood education program that offered our children stability, continuity, safety, enriching experiences and opportunities, and the loving support of extended family and community. Our work to nurture and bring healing conditions to the children was strengthened by our work to support the mothers and families.

Nearly every family Sophia Project served was headed by a young single mother trying to stabilize while experiencing high and sustained levels of stress. Typically she was unable to meet the needs of her young children. It might take several years for a young mother in such circumstances to gain the capacities needed to nurture her children and stabilize her family. It is critical that the needs of the young children are met during this time in order to give them the best possible chance of success in school and in later life.

Our work was based on our conviction that healthy early childhood development is the essential foundation for a strong, caring, capable adult. Sophia Project's programming was shaped by research that has shown that, for disadvantaged children, only the most intensive models have measurable positive effects on children in the short and long term, and the measured effects of the most intensive interventions are substantial.

By any standard the Sophia Project model was very intensive. We had a child-to-staff ratio of 3 to 1, and our work was anchored in a full-time live-in community located where our families lived.

Small, even subtle changes at the beginning of a life can have a very significant impact in later life. While we endeavored to document and celebrate all successes, we knew that the true impact of our work would likely only be seen years in the future. As stated in the High/Scope Perry Preschool forty-year longitudinal study, "high-quality preschool programs for young children living in poverty contribute to their intellectual and social development in childhood and their school success, economic performance, and reduced commission of crime in adulthood. This study confirms that these findings extend not only to young adults, but also to adults in midlife."[1] More research supporting work at Sophia Project can be found below in "Gauging the Effectiveness of Sophia Project."

Although our primary focus was on the children, Sophia Project also intensively supported parents. When a mother first arrived with her children, they were often in a state of extreme chaos. In response, the Sophia Project staff immediately crafted a family support plan to meet the specific needs of each family. This plan provided reliable support while they negotiated the transition from chaos to a stable and healthy family life. By creating community with our families, children and mothers had a safe and nurturing space to develop the skills necessary for their age and circumstances.

The need to include substantial family support is confirmed by a study from Harvard University's Center on The Developing Child that included several program effectiveness factors, particularly pertaining to children from low- and very-low-income families. Sophia Project practiced all of these effectiveness factors including pairing parental support with high-quality early childhood education and intensive services that met the specific needs of children experiencing toxic levels of stress. The study confirmed the pivotal importance of enriched experiences in early childhood: "Early experiences determine whether a child's developing brain architecture provides a strong or weak foundation for all future learning, behavior and health."[2]

Sophia Project education and development programs were based on Rudolf Steiner's indications regarding early childhood education, tailored to address the unique needs of our children. The live-in community, working out of the teachings of Karl König and the practices of a Camphill community, created a nurturing, home-like environment and provided the possibility of 24-hour availability to meet the urgent needs of families.

We had two homes: Sophia House for children age three to five, and Myrtle House for children age birth to three. Our programs included:

1. Early childhood education program
2. Before-and-after-school program
3. Infant and toddler development program
4. Overnight weekend respite care program serving the children and families who had completed the daily programs
5. Parent education and family support program
6. Festival celebrations and artistic activities

Families generally participated in two to three years of intensive daily services designed to meet individual needs, followed by services that lessened in intensity over the following five years. The key to our success was the continuity of our programs.

Although some children stayed later, the weekday programs operated Monday through Friday, from 6:00 a.m. until 6:30 p.m. We scheduled overnight respite care for children every other weekend, Friday afternoon through noon Sunday. We offered additional overnight and extended hours as needed.

In addition to children and families participating in neighborhood activities or festival celebrations, each month Sophia Project served 65 children plus their mothers and siblings. Once both houses were open, twenty-seven children participated in the daily programs. The other children utilized emergency and overnight respite services on weekends and occasional weekday nights or participated in outings or artistic workshops.

Sophia Project Newsletter, 2003

Jessica, four years old, and her mother Lee, have experienced abuse and torment bordering on torture. Much of this violence has erupted at the dinner table. Jessica arrives understandably in a wild and frightened state, unable to sit still, darting from place to place, crying frequently. Over time, with a safe environment, beauty and order, consistent limits and a chance to play, Jessica is beginning to calm down. She is afraid of the Jack-in-the-Box but asks every day to play with it. She asks an adult to tell her when it will pop up. Watching from across the room, and then slowly closer, she now sometimes turns the handle herself. She is determined to learn to cope with the surprise of the Jack-in-the-Box. Next is the tea set: day after day she sets the table and brings several dolls to sit at the table. The teachers are near-by ready to join, assist, or stay away as needed. Jessica herself seems almost ready to sit at the table that she sets with such solemnity and care.

Endnotes

1. Lawrence J. Schweinhart, Ph. D., "HighScope Perry Preschool Study Through Age 40: Summary, Conclusions, and FAQs" (link to document at www.highscope.org/research/online-resources,), page 5.

2. Center on the Developing Child, "A Science-Based Framework for Early Childhood Policy: Using Evidence to Improve Outcomes in Learning, Behavior, and Health for Vulnerable Children," http://developingchild.harvard.edu."

Daily Programs

Early Childhood Education

Waldorf early childhood education is sometimes described as receiving the children from the spirit and guiding them into the goodness of earthly life. Our children desperately needed both parts of this ideal process.

The children arrived each morning between 6:00 and 7:00 a.m. After washing and often changing into clean, warm clothes, most children enjoyed a warm breakfast, which was available long enough to accommodate every arrival time. The children developed and learned through living life together in a rich environment of beauty, order, and harmony. Among many other activities, the children played, baked, gardened, painted, molded beeswax, sang, celebrated festivals, helped with the cooking, listened and were listened to, looked at books, danced, drew, and helped clean up. When outside time was over they washed (in warm water everyday, for some an uncommon comfort and luxury), listened to a story, and ate their main meal of the day, a warm nutritious lunch. Then each child went to his or her own cot, happy to have a cozy nap before the afternoon activities began.

Afternoons had a different character. Usually led by someone experienced in creating a nourishing home, the afternoons and evenings were based on Camphill understandings and principles as applied in a home, distinct from a classroom.[1] In addition to benefiting from this healing environment, the children had the opportunity to see coworkers who had a leading role in the morning, fill a supporting role (such as cleaning or dishwashing) in the afternoon, thereby honoring and ennobling all daily life and its many and varied tasks.

Young children learn largely through imitation, taking in and forming themselves from what lives around them.[2] This places an enormous responsibility on teachers and all those who guide young children to be worthy of imitation. Rudolf Steiner urged teachers to focus not only on what we do but also on who we are.

The children's mothers were often dismayed when learning about the power of imitation, regularly stating that they did not want their children to imitate them. It was important to gently help them realize that their young child would also imitate their mother's striving. They would imitate their mother's persistence in the face of enormous obstacles. Their child would likely also need this capacity. We tried to help

Sophia Project Newsletter, 2005

When Luis, 3 years old, arrived in January he and his family were still struggling with homelessness. His mother was overwhelmed with the care of her other child, a ten-year-old handicapped girl, and was unable to do more than meet Luis's basic needs. They had all experienced domestic violence. It took consistent careful guidance for Luis to learn to trust others and to interact with the other children without hitting. After a half year he is much more peaceful and has found his way through the trauma. He spends a lot of time on the swings singing. With his arms extended to the side to hold onto the swing, it is easy to see his disfigured arm, which healed poorly after it was broken in a violent incident--a painful reminder of what he and many of our children endure. Less visible but equally powerful are the inner capacities Luis is now building which enable him to wait for a turn on the beloved swing, ask for help for a starting push and immerse himself in the swinging movement and in his joyful (and quite loud) song: "The Itsy-Bitsy Spider went up the waterspout. Down came the rain and washed the spider out. Out came the sun and dried up all the rain, and the Itsy-Bitsy Spider went up the spout again." Perhaps Luis recognizes some of his own tenacity in the spider he sings about with such enthusiasm.

each mother understand that her struggle was profoundly worthy of imitation; in this way she was the very best teacher.

By virtue of being human we all have the potential for an enriching relationship to other human beings, color, form, music, story, the elements of earth, fire, water, and air, the kingdoms of nature, and to the cosmic world. All of this belongs to every human being regardless of social situation or economic standing. Because our children and mothers had been living with constant fear and high levels of stress, they had little inner space or time to cultivate these relationships.

Alarmingly, our children did not feel they were a part of the world. As they developed these relationships, they begin to feel more secure in knowing that they do belong. Mothers too began to know this for their children and for themselves. This knowing is a support for connectedness and diminishes isolation; families and individuals experiencing isolation are susceptible to breaking apart.

We took care to consistently include the quality of wholeness. For example, a star or a horse would not be displayed on a shelf without context: we would be sure to put a horse in a meadow or a star surrounded by a night sky. For our children, whose experiences were very fragmented, it was especially important to put objects and events in a meaningful context. Drawings that show, for example, not only a tree but also the ground from which it grows and the sky surrounding it, stories told from beginning to end, activities that include preparation, the work itself, and clean up, all offer the quality of wholeness. Wholeness begins the repair of shattered fragments of learning and experience.

Stories were carefully chosen with an awareness that the children's life experiences were often cruelly concrete. They were very awake, rarely dreamy as many young children in less threatening circumstance usually are. Stories that suggested, even indirectly, that in the end good people get what they need, perhaps food and comfort, while the bad people remain hungry, were very distressing and confusing for the children. Other stories, such as Santa Claus giving presents to good girls and boys, indirectly told the children that they were bad. After all, Santa had not left them toys on Christmas morning. In contrast, appropriate stories brought healing satisfaction, and inspired hours of play.

Children's play is vital to their well-being.[3] This deeply integrating activity engenders emotional security, cognitive and physical strength, joy, and laughter, and helps the child work out frustrations and anxieties. Nourishing and protecting the children's play was always a priority. It frequently took time for new children's creative play to awaken. A child may initially need to play with an adult or engage in activities that rely less on inner activity, such as making snack. Coworkers needed to be very sensitive to the nuances of each child's situation, engaging, protecting, intervening, observing, or encouraging as needed.

The children's lives outside of Sophia House were very different from the way of being we encouraged at Sophia House. Two absolute rules were (1) no gunplay, and (2) no hurting, hitting, shoving, or pushing of any kind. We said, for example, "There is no hitting at Sophia House." It was important to phrase it this way; we did not say, "There is no hitting," as there may well be hitting in their home environment. In this and in many aspects of Sophia House, children and coworkers learned to understand that, although something may not be true at home, it was true here. The children were learning another language, another way of being. We did not deny their experiences outside of Sophia House; we did not say that it was wrong, only that it was not done here.

Coworkers needed to be aware when a child's play was of benefit and when it became destructive. For example, one day a three-year old girl had witnessed a shooting on the street. The man, bleeding and unconscious, just laid there, no one came to help him. The little girl was understandably very upset. Using several of the standing puppets, she played out the scene over and over. Each time no one came to help. At a certain point, her tone began to harden. This was the sign that a new possibility, a new story, was needed. I sat down next to her and asked if I could play. When she assented I took another puppet, and when she reached the part of the story when no one helped, my puppet came to help. "No," she said, "That is not what happened." " I know," I said, "but this time it will be different and there will be help." "It's not like that," she protested. "I know, but let's make a new story." We made a story that had help and care. She then began to use my puppet herself and tell the new story. Warmth returned to her body and to her expression. She continued to play for a while longer and then skipped away to play something else.

There were also times when normal guidelines needed to be suspended. Generally, the children were expected to share the toys. However, there could be exceptions. When Gloria arrived she was sad and listless. Unimaginably heartbreaking, she had been sexually abused at this very young age. For weeks she did not play. Then she began to gather toys around herself, making a kind of barrier. She sat within the circle, which was made of many toys. Naturally children wanted to play with some of the toys, and they repeatedly pointed out that Gloria was not playing with them but just keeping them. Hoarding toys was generally not allowed. Teachers and interns explained that Gloria was using them in her own way and that we needed to let her have them. We made sure that no one took them or in any way crossed the boundary Gloria had made. After several days, some children gently asked Gloria if they might play with a toy if they didn't take it away from her circle. That seemed to be all right with her. Little by little the boundary, having served its purpose, became softer and the little one within seemed to regain some security in knowing it could be controlled. Gloria went on to be a leader in many creative enactments of long stories. Sometimes she would need to be reminded that now she needed to share the toys. Usually she considered that a reasonable request and would, with a young child's knowing smile, share.

Some children required the attention of mental health specialists. Because the children were with us for so many hours each day, the work that in other circumstances might have been done at home by parents was done at Sophia House. The specialists were invariably impressed with the work at Sophia House and expressed the hope that other clients could have a space at Sophia House.

Five-Year-Old Work

Teachers prepared the children who would be attending public kindergarten in the fall through special "five-year-old work." For forty-five minutes a day beginning in April, the children worked on writing their name, recognizing the letters and numbers, and becoming familiar with worksheets similar to the ones they would encounter in school. Subsequently the children managed well in public kindergartens.

Saturday School

An important ingredient in keeping our children and families stable was our ability to craft programs that met their emerging needs. A large group of children graduated from the daily 3- to 5-year-old program in June 2008 and began public kindergarten that fall. In order to maintain the self-confidence the children gained while in our daily programs, we gave our kindergarten children a great deal of support, usually on an individual basis. Because of the large group of kindergarteners in 2008, we started a new program, Saturday School. By meeting their developmental needs, Saturday School helped ensure the children's future success in public school.

Sophia Project Newsletter, 2010

Saturday School encourages our kindergarten children to use their imagination and reconnect to their creativity. The children are eager for these experiences as their weekday schools offer little opportunity for this kind of activity. When the children arrive in the morning they are happy to see one another and the Sophia Project adults. The children are usually a bit rambunctious at the start of the day but soon the rich world of imagination opens up and they become engrossed in their play. They happily flow with the familiar rhythm of inside and outside play, singing, circle games, arts, baking, and nutritious meals and snacks. By the end of the day the children are rosy cheeked and have regained their vibrancy.

On our last Saturday School we took nine children to the local indoor ice skating rink. For most of the children this would be their first time. There was a mixture of excitement and apprehension among the group as we prepared to leave for the rink. Once everyone was suited up with ice skates we began to venture out onto the ice in small groups. The temperaments of our children shone through as each took their own approach to this very foreign experience. Some held on happily to the wall content to scoot inch by inch and get a feel for the ice. Some clung desperately to the hands of an adult while others were determined to go alone.

Whatever the approach, every child experienced the inevitable falls that are part of the process of learning to skate on ice. Every single one got up again and again and again. Some welcomed the assistance of a nearby adult. One child, Lisa, asked, "Are you going to help me every time I fall?" and seemed to be relieved to hear the answer, "Of course." Others refused a helping hand, determined to find their way back up on their own. By the end of our skating session each child had made huge strides in their ability to ice skate. In the last moments on the ice we heard chorus of "Teacher, look at me!" accompanied by huge, proud smiles.

The children have grown strong despite early childhood experiences of homelessness, violence, fear and deep poverty. They have shown over and over again that a wise education within a caring community can heal their trauma and nurture their healthy development. Their ice skating efforts are a picture of this. They may fall many times but they have shown how willing they are to get back up and try again. Their resilience is inspiring.

Jen Ventura, former coworker

Before-and-After-School Program

The before-and-after school program served children in kindergarten through grade 3. After a good breakfast and a bit of play the school age children checked their backpacks to see that they had everything they needed for the day, dressed for the weather, and walked or rode to school with a coworker. After school, at about 2:00 p.m., a coworker waited to pick them up and listened with interest as the children talked about their day. Snack was followed by homework and tutoring, story or artistic activity, and outside play. Between 6:00 and 6:30 p.m., after late snack, the children were picked up. Regular attendance, nutritious food, daily help with homework, coworker support of parents' participation in conferences at their child's school, and much-appreciated school supplies resulted in positive school experiences, so different from that of many school children in our neighborhood.

One child, age 7, wrote a story about her walk from Sophia House to school: "The birds fly so happy in the sky and the sky is blue and the sun is bright. I am on my way to school. I have my backpack, my pencils, my homework, my sharpener, my books and my eraser and that is in my backpack. "

Beginning in 2005 we offered a before-school program in Myrtle House for children in grade 5 through middle school who had graduated from the Sophia Project early childhood program or had siblings in the program. These children arrived early in order to receive help with homework, eat a nutritious breakfast, and, for those attending parochial school, pick up a packed lunch.

Infant and Toddler Program

With the opening of Myrtle House in 2005, Sophia Project realized the goal of creating a separate program for infants and toddlers within a setting specifically designed to meet their needs. The chaos, stress, and fear created by frequent moving from place to place, unsafe surroundings that restricted crawling or touching, an extremely stressed mother, broken rhythms of sleeping, eating and playing, poor nutrition, and exposure to violence were replaced with rhythm, peace, beauty, warmth, and a safe, nurturing environment.

This program offered each young mother in our community a trusted place to learn how to care for her child through individualized participation in the program, and a safe place to leave her baby or toddler. In addition to practical skills, the mothers gained an appreciation of the importance of the first years of life.

Individual sessions with mothers, as well as group trainings with coworkers, included the following topics:

- Newborn children do not discriminate between self and world.
- Nurture and bonding are the basis for the establishment of the baby's trust in the world.
- Autonomy in the second year is built on the trust established in the first year.
- Foundations for speech are laid down in the child's first year.
- Speech and movement develop in relation to each other.
- Movement and balance develop in relation to each other.
- Security is conveyed through touch, warmth, physical and emotional contact, and healthy rhythms of bodily functions such as sleeping and eating.
- If a child is not comforted when distressed, the child can become disheartened and discouraged and begin to form a barrier separating him- or herself from the environment.

- A child learns gradually through a process of imitation.

- To the extent that the child's development is compromised through trauma or neglect, the child's capacity to imitate may be damaged.

- Symptoms of regression can include issues with eating, disturbed sleep patterns, loss of speech, loss of bowel control, and loss of the ability to play.

- The importance of free exploration and crawling on the floor in a safe environment.

- The importance of games through which a child develops. For example, through "Peek a Boo" a child can develop tolerance for separation for a short time and the security that gratification is not far away.

- The vitally important role of the primary caregivers.

Observation and record keeping for the infants and toddlers was very detailed and included checklists for social, emotional, physical, and cognitive developmental milestones. In special need cases these checklists and milestones were created in consultation with the child's physician. Diaries were kept for each infant or toddler. These diaries, shared daily with the mothers, detailed the child's activities, including eating, drinking, sleeping, toilet training or diaper changes, changes of clothes, indoor and outdoor activities, and any other important information.

Naturally, all coworkers were responsible for the well-being of all the children, but the primary needs of each infant or toddler were the responsibility of only two adults and the child's mother.

~

The Rain Never Diminishes Toddler Play
Sophia Project Newsletter, 2009

The rain never diminishes the toddlers' desire to go outside and play. Within our fenced in yards are gardens, trees, grassy areas, hills, sandboxes, and outside toys. On rainy days the children suit up in rain pants, thick warm coats, hats, warm socks and rain boots.

Often the walkways are hidden below enormously inviting puddles and the less grassy parts of the yard have become pleasingly squishy mud. Wiggling worms, becoming visible as they are flooded out of their earthen caverns, fill the children with wonder. The children spend hours scooping water into buckets from the puddles and scooping mud into pails. They also enjoy going fishing in the larger "lake-size" puddles and catching all sorts of imaginary fish.

Coming inside they delight in squeaking their boots on the linoleum floor. They change into dry clothes, scrub the mud off of their hands and transition into the cozy indoors while their outdoor play clothes tumble in the driers and the clouds outside unfurl the next puddle-making rainy time.

Many of our children live in tight quarters with their families without access to safe outdoor play areas, or they have parents who do not often have the possibility to take their children to parks. For this reason the morning and afternoon outside times at Myrtle House are a vital chance for the children to develop a connection to nature and the outside world and to practice important gross motor skills like running and jumping. Each season offers unique opportunities in the yard.

Becky Rowland, former coworker

~

Toddler Goodness and Compassion
Sophia Project Newsletter, 2009

Amid the shouts of "mine!" and "no!" that ring through the toddler room, great acts of compassion can also be seen.

Alicia, a 22-month-old girl, upset and crying was called into the arms of Lily, not quite two years old. Lily consoled Alicia, patting her back and holding her. After a few minutes Alicia, through her tears, looked at Lily and politely said "more please," Lily held her a bit longer. The compassion shown by Lily is particularly remarkable because Lily's family is currently experiencing some painful interpersonal instability. Lily's ability to reach out of herself and offer help to another even though she herself is feeling vulnerable is a living picture of one of the capacities we attempt to build in the children, and in ourselves.

Over time, the children at Myrtle House come to understand that their needs will be met. They have a predictable rhythm; they know what is coming next. They see adults caring for the children, one another, and their environment with love and warmth. Through witnessing and being a part of these processes, the children experience a growing sense of comfort and security. This allows them to participate more fully in the world. They are able to take in what happens around them, have an inner experience, and sometimes an outer response, as Lily did when she saw that Alicia needed to be held.

In this way our work goes beyond the scope of the specific families we serve. Goodness will generate more goodness and compassion will help generate a sense of care for the other. These children and mothers can now be an inspiration to others for healing and transforming.

Sarah Deurloo, former coworker

Respite Care Program

The overnight respite care program for children operated every other weekend, Friday night through noon Sunday. When needed, we offered additional overnight care. In emergencies, such as episodes of domestic violence, families stayed with us for a week or two. The program took place in both houses. Sophia House had a big room that slept five children. The smaller setting in Myrtle House met the needs of the most vulnerable families, including children's preteen and teen siblings who were sometimes on suicide watch.

In the first years of Sophia Project we offered respite care to young single mothers staying at Raphael House shelter. Homeless mothers and children are subject to high levels of stress for which they are ill equipped, and as a result may reach a breaking point leading to child neglect or abuse. Respite care is one of the most effective tools for preventing child neglect and abuse. Because the children and families receiving respite care knew and trusted the Sophia House staff, the mothers could truly relax, knowing their children were safe. The children joyfully experienced the rhythm of dinner at a big table, baths, stories, and bedtime. They also enjoyed games, outings, and artistic activities.

Several families living with chronic high stress received respite care at regular intervals over several years. For these children, coming to Sophia House was like an old-fashioned visit to grandma's. They bounded up the stairs, chose their bed, found their doll or toy, made sure all their favorite things were still there, checked on the growth of the plants in the garden, and settled into a deliciously predictable weekend. One child who came regularly for eight years once remarked with amazement, "At Sophia House everyone always waits with you at dinner until you are finished." She sighed, "You are never going to move, right?" She valued having a touchstone in her otherwise chaotic life. That little girl still contacts us regularly. In 2018 she will graduate from college.

After Sophia Project's first three years, respite care continued for only those Raphael House families whom we had identified as especially benefiting from repeated visits. We no longer provided the one-time respite care for Raphael House families. Instead of serving Raphael House families, we began providing respite care for the children who had completed their years in the Sophia Project daily programs.

Festivals, Outings, and Artistic Activity

Children are deeply nourished by engaging in the great rhythm of the seasons and the traditions of yearly festivals. At Sophia Project the first festival of the new school year was Michaelmas, celebrated in September. The children resonated with the powerful story of St. George who with the aid of the archangel Michael overcomes and transforms the dragon. At circle time the children took turns playing every character in a dramatization of the story. Throughout the year during free play they frequently created new, mostly modern-day stories, in which evil was transformed usually with the help of Michael or St. George.

Early in October the children began discussing what they would be for Halloween. Two weeks before Halloween each child had a chance to try on any of the costumes in our costume box. They relished knowing what costume they and their friends would wear on the party day. They enjoyed living into their character in a safe, predictable environment. For our children, being a part of the preparation brought satisfaction and the joy of anticipation. They did not have a positive relationship to surprise; this was probably because the experience of surprise was too close to their negative experience of chaos.

Children who had "graduated" from our programs often came back to borrow a costume. This was sometimes because they did not have access to one, but more often it was to try to rekindle the magic associated with the costumes. As one child put it, "I want to be a real lion." After the children went home in the evening, Halloween trick-or-treating started in the neighborhood. We regularly had over ninety children at both of the houses.

Every child joyfully anticipated his or her birthday celebration; it was a cherished special day. The birthday child helped make the cake and decorate the birthday table. Wearing a crown and a cape, the child entered a hushed room where friends were quietly sitting. When possible the child's family also attended. Singing, "In heaven shines a golden star, an angel brought me from afar . . . " the teacher led the child around the birthday table and then told the birthday story of a little angel that came over the rainbow bridge to the earth. Each child gave the birthday child one of the specially wrapped gifts; all the children clapped with delight as each gift was opened.

Sophia Project Newsletter, 2007

I visited Sophia Project the weekend before Christmas, when respite festivities were in full swing. Stopping first at Myrtle House, I found Carol and David along with a board member and her partner playing with Dorothy, of 18 months, who along with her brothers and sister had spent the previous night at Myrtle House. Dorothy's two brothers, age four and six, along with her sister who was eight, were all at Fairyland with the interns, along with two other children from different families.

The board member and her partner had just delivered four new bicycles. Three of them for a family who had "graduated" and were now living in Hayward. The fourth bike was for the oldest son of a different family returning to Honduras in January. With the bike he would now be able to ride to the local school, making it possible for him to finish high school. David would be delivering them to the Moms of these children so that they would be able to give them as their gift on Christmas Day.

Carol and I went to Sophia House where some interns and all the rest of the children were playing happily while they waited for a home-made pizza dinner and an evening of tree trimming and cookies the children had made that afternoon. It was a joy to see these children I had known when they were so much younger, now so well, clear and healthy.

Ellie Wood, board member

Although the celebration of new life at Easter time and the joy of summer at St. John's time each had their cherished traditions, Christmas was the most dear to the children's hearts. Beginning with the Advent spiral we celebrated the coming of the child of light with many preparations including, baking, crafts, gift making, and tree decorating.

Most of the mothers in the daily program could not manage Christmas celebrations at home but happily participated in celebrations at Sophia Project, especially the children's concert. Federica (Flicka) von Stade, world-renowned mezzo-soprano, was a Sophia Project board member. Each Christmas she taught the children several Christmas carols and then accompanied them in the Christmas concert for parents. The mothers were always deeply touched by the beauty of the performance. It was important for the children and mothers to experience themselves as co-creators of beauty and special moments. Equally important was the opportunity to be the one giving a gift. Every mother received a Christmas gift for herself as well as specially chosen gifts for her to give to her children on Christmas.

During Advent the children experienced building up the nativity scene with Mary and Joseph coming closer and closer and finally arriving at the stable. On that day we built a large Christmas cave out of stars and blue cloth that encompassed the candle-lit nativity scene, and a present for each child and coworker. After hearing the Christmas story, one child stepped into the cave, chose a gift, and gave it to the person whose name was written on the tag. That person would then go into the cave and choose a gift, and so it would continue until each person had a gift. Giving a gift was a valuable experience for every child. We then opened them and played together. Depending on the toy chosen for the child, it was very important for a coworker to play with the child in order to help the child build a relationship to their new toy and help with necessary instructions or putting it together.

The children did not have Christmas trees at home. Sophia Project had three Christmas trees, one in Myrtle House for the toddlers, one downstairs in Sophia House for the early childhood program, which was lovingly adorned with multitudes of decorations made by the children, and one upstairs in the Sophia House respite space. We had many children for respite care during the Christmas season. They all cherished the experience of baking cookies or making gingerbread houses, going on outings, snuggling on the sofa during a Christmas movie, and especially decorating the tree. Staff and interns would un-decorate the tree after each group of respite children left, so the next group could trim the tree and unwrap the gifts they found there the next morning.

Throughout the year we had many outings designed for specific age groups. Outings created relationships to the seasons of the year and the beauty of the natural world; they also formed a foundation for cultural literacy. Outings included:

- Regular outings: to the beach, lake, streams, forest, parks of all sizes, zoo, mountains, and botanical gardens
- Seasonal outings: to the pumpkin patch, to see Christmas lights, and to the farm
- Activity outings: to Children's Fairyland, bowling, ice-skating, mini-golf, and bike riding
- Artistic Outings: to the ballet, galleries, concerts, and plays
- Outings to experience transportation: trains, ferry rides, ships, the port, and the reservoir

For preteens and teens, we had special days for artistic work because they no longer had the opportunity to engage in art. They were eager to deepen their relationship to color, form, music, drama, and literature. Artistic work is transformative and therapeutic; it brings joy and satisfaction. It can build inner strength and flexibility; it simultaneously engages physical, emotional, and cognitive faculties. Few activities in today's world call for this sort of total engagement. It was a great pleasure to make art days available.

Endnotes

1. See, for example, Veronica van Duin, *Homemaking as a Social Art* (Forest Row, UK: Rudolf Steiner Press, 2000).

2. See, for example, Rudolf Steiner, *The Child's Changing Consciousness and Waldorf Education* (Hudson, NY: The Anthroposophic Press, 1988).

3. See, for example, Sally Jenkinson, (Stroud, UK: Hawthorn Press, 2001).

Sophia Project Newsletter, 2012

One thing I remember is how sweet and loving everyone was at Sophia House. My experience here was wonderful. When I came to Sophia House it felt like home, it wasn't just a program. I could be myself here. I just loved everything about it. I love how on our birthdays we get gifts or go out with someone from the house.

I remember at the end of every year we would gather up with everyone that was a part of Sophia House at one point in time. I love to meet everyone and I love just the fact that we would all enjoy ourselves. We would spend the whole day together from 10:00 a.m. to 5:00 p.m. at the beach. All the little children and the older kids just enjoyed the time we spent together.

Another time was [my sister's] quinceñera (fifteenth birthday). Windsong and I spent two weeks, or maybe a month, making her cake. I really loved baking with Windsong. We made the cake three times to make it just right for the day of the party. At the end the cake was wonderful. It looked very beautiful and it tasted delicious.

My time at Sophia House was the best part of my life. Everyone here really brought me joy. I don't think I would be half the person I am today without them. I really want to say thank you for being there for me and my family when we needed you most.

Belinda, high school sophomore

Family Support Program

It was crucial that the coworkers consistently held a picture of what each mother in our care was capable of, even if she was not manifesting that capability in a given moment. This created a mood of possibility, encouragement, and trust, enabling our mothers to grasp opportunities for growth. Mothers learned, for example, that if one is not feeling well, one must find a way to still work but leave some things for another day, instead of missing work altogether or becoming sicker from pushing too hard. Mothers also learned that mistakes, backsliding, and fear are a part of the journey and can be overcome. The effort required to overcome mistakes manifested in big and small ways, including: knowing that if one burns a meal it does not mean that one cannot cook, missing an appointment does not make one an unreliable person, and even longing to see an abusive ex-partner does not mean one cannot make good choices. Burdened by many wounding and difficult experiences, the mothers regularly experienced a misstep as a complete failure. They needed people around them who knew them at their best, and also when they were struggling. This fuller perception helped our mothers learn how to call on strong parts of themselves, maintain their level of growth, and move forward even in difficult moments. Working with Rudolf Steiner's "Faithfulness" verse helped the coworkers practice this way of perceiving the mothers and each other:

> Create for yourself a new, indomitable perception of faithfulness.
> What is usually called faithfulness passes so quickly.
> Let this be your faithfulness:
> You will experience moments . . . fleeting moments . . . with the other person.
> The human being will appear to you then as if filled,
> irradiated with the archetype of his spirit.
> And then there may be . . . indeed will be . . . other moments,
> long periods of time, when human beings are darkened.
> But you will learn to say to yourself at such times: "The spirit makes me strong. I remember the archetype. I saw it once.
> No illusion, no deception shall rob me of it."
> Always struggle for the image you saw. This struggle is faithfulness.
> Striving thus for faithfulness, we shall be close to one another,
> as if endowed with the protective powers of angels.

I met with every mother who wanted to join Sophia Project to explain the program's requirements and to discuss her wishes and goals for herself and her children. Mothers needed to commit themselves to working on their goals and to participating fully in the program. Most of our mothers were newly self-sufficient and recovering from homelessness; others were on the brink of homelessness. Mothers in the program had be working, looking for work, or attending school. (Exceptions were made for those in mental health or recovery programs.) Mothers needed to be clean and sober at the time of enrollment.

Because our mothers needed what money they earned for rent and food, there was no fee for the program. Some of the mothers qualified for a two-year childcare stipend from Catholic Charities, but Sophia Project did not take the stipend. Instead, we arranged for the stipend to be put in escrow until the mother and child completed the Sophia Project daily programs. The mother could then use that money to pay for childcare and after-school expenses she would incur once the family was no longer part of Sophia Project's daily programs. This helped support the family's continued stability.

If Sophia Project was a good match for the mother, and there was space in the program for her children, the family began immediately. During their first weeks mothers and children participated in activities together. Soon the mother and her children felt safe, a sign that healing had begun.

Throughout the family's time at Sophia Project, I would regularly meet the mother to review timelines and steps toward the mother's goals. For our mothers, the road to stability tended to be rocky and unpredictable. The fear of falling into desperation again weighed heavily upon them. Typically, mothers in our program were in their early twenties and had few job skills, low self-esteem, and little education. Many needed time to see themselves as an asset to their family and the source of potential solutions. Often it was difficult for them to imagine a different life or to visualize the steps needed to accomplish a goal. For many mothers, being a part of the Sophia Project community meant that the coworkers held the pieces of her life together as she worked with a few pieces at a time, slowly but steadily learning to manage them all.

From their first day onward children typically insisted on coming every day to Sophia Project. This was an important support for the mothers, especially at the beginning of their time in the program. For working parents it meant not missing work. For parents still involved with recovery from addiction it meant keeping a regular schedule and meeting daily commitments, a key aspect of recovery.

Very few of the mothers grew up in a functioning home. In order to create one themselves they needed to experience a warm, well-ordered home. We were intentionally a licensed childcare home, not a childcare center, so that the children could experience a nurturing home and the mothers could see and practice homemaking, including creating and celebrating holidays and birthdays, eating as a family, conversing with one another, and learning to care for and trust one another. These life skill lessons cannot easily be programmed. They are most effective when they take place as situations arise in everyday life. For this reason the mothers' participation in our daily lives was critical to their healing, especially in the first year or two. For one day per week, a half-day per week, or as work permitted, mothers accompanied their children in programs that were rich in culture, artistic work, literature, song, and activities in nature. This helped them to build relationships to cultural riches and to enriching experiences in nature. Through participating in the Sophia House activities the mothers could take into their own family culture such practices as good communication, festival celebration, story time, nutritious meals, family activities, and age-appropriate discipline.

The Sophia Project live-in community served as an extended family for the children and mothers, offering intangible and less programmable support as well as 24/7 support in emergency situations. When a mother started a new job, the hours were often difficult. She did not have sick days or benefits. This often meant a long process of "paying her dues" that included being on call every and any day, for six months to a year. For a young mother on her own with small children this is an impossible situation. A person in this situation needs support to be successful.

Each family situation was unique, requiring an individual support plan. Plans sometimes included helping a mother learn about nutrition by going food shopping with her, cooking at her home, or having her be a part of the cooking at Sophia House. Other support plans included learning to mend or alter clothes on the sewing machine or assistance with home improvements. Affordable housing was often substandard, but with support and guidance the mothers succeeded in making their homes warm, attractive, functional, and a nurturing place for their children.

Family support plans could also include helping our mothers advocate for appropriate social services, look for work, locate mental health and medical care, apply for special services, or file forms or paperwork. Sophia Project provided food, household items, clothing, Christmas and birthday presents, and occasional help with rent, bus passes, or gas and electric bills. Some mothers needed tutoring in order to pass a test or practice interviewing for a job. Effective family support required being available to the mothers for guidance on family relationships and responding to requests for advice and referrals of all kinds.

Our mothers were often intimidated by or fearful of the public school system. They required help to understand the expectations of their child's school, especially in regard to parental support of their child's academic progress. Coworkers sometimes accompanied our mothers to parent-teacher conferences. In time, every mother in the program became able to handle this important responsibility.

Some of our families lived nearby and could walk to Sophia House. Most families struggled with the cost of public transportation. Some mothers came to the West Oakland BART station with their children, passed their children over a fence to a coworker, and then returned home on the BART, thereby avoiding the cost of the return fare. (The children were lifted over at a place in the fence that could not easily be seen by the BART ticket collectors. The ticket collectors were always very accommodating, taking care to not look our way.) To help our the mothers get to work on time, coworkers also picked children up at public bus stops. The children got off the bus and their mother continued on her journey, making it possible for her to avoid walking to Sophia House, returning to the bus stop, and waiting for the next bus.

Even with these accommodations, some families could not afford transportation. David picked up those children every morning and took then home again in the evening. In the first year of Sophia Project, one of these children was living with her mother in a halfway house for people struggling with mental health issues. We worked with the family's Child Protective Service social worker, who observed the marked improvement in both mother and child, and subsequently referred additional mothers and children.

Child development and parenting education were central to every family support plan. Every mother participated with me in frequent, in-depth conversations on child development paired with practical application. Because many mothers feared being harshly judged for their lack of parenting skills, these conversations were individual and confidential. Conversation topics included managing behavior; knowing when to intervene in a child's behavior; the effective practices of redirecting and time-outs; understanding that over-indulgence can lead to difficult behavior; eliminating scare tactics (such as: "if you don't listen the police will take you away"); and the negative consequences of spanking, hitting, pinching, or twisting.

After being guided to a clear picture of their child's physical, mental, and emotional development, mothers were much more able to meet their child's specific needs. As their children became more manageable, mothers had more opportunities to play and share delight with their children, and had the satisfaction of reaching the parenting goals they had set for themselves.

In addition to individual conversations, the following topics were discussed in occasional group settings:

- A regular predictable schedule helps the child to be calmer and easier to manage. This includes a regular early bedtime.
- Small children especially need to be kept warm on cold days.
- A healthy child is easier to manage.
- Consistent guidelines and rules are very important.
- Young children learn from what we do, not so much from what we say. Model good habits.
- Each child needs a few minutes a day with her mother that is just for her.
- The importance of looking at books or reading every evening with their child.
- TV can lead to chaotic behavior.

Working with the mothers required vigilance, clarity, and sensitivity to their vulnerable inner and outer state. The interns were usually about the same age as the mothers but with very different life experiences that had not prepared them to understand or advise the mothers. Intern training included careful coaching on how to respond to the mothers, usually involving listening respectfully and saying, "I will let Carol know." Until 2009, mothers worked almost exclusively with me. In 2009, Tracy Weber joined Sophia Project. Tracy was older than the mothers and possessed the inner capacities and outer skills to work with them successfully. Tracy continued to work with the Sophia Project families until 2014. She is now a social worker and has developed a successful residential program for mothers struggling with substance abuse, and their children ages birth to three.

Sophia Project developed two financial programs for family support. First, we offered short-term no-interest loans to parents facing unexpected reduced income or emergency expenses. Families did not have cash on hand to pay a large bill in a timely fashion but could pay back these loans if given a little time. This program relieved a great deal of pressure and anxiety, enabling our mothers to focus on their children and their work. These small loans were always completely repaid.

Secondly, we established a college fund. Many parents saved ten dollars a month, which was initially matched by generous Camphill Beaver Run coworkers. The amount seems modest, but by the time these young children were eighteen it was enough for them to enroll in community college. As of February 2017, fifteen Sophia Project children are in college; the first will graduate in June 2017.

Equally important was the impact the college fund had on the families at the time. The children who were old enough to understand were delighted that they would be going to college, that magical place many interns had recently attended. It also had a major impact on the self-esteem of the mothers. With tears in her eyes, one of the mothers said, "It's hard to believe we are a family that's saving for college."

~

Everyone at Sophia House has Shaped Me in Some Way
Sophia Project Newsletter, 2009

Being at Sophia House has opened up so many opportunities for me as a person. I entered Sophia House when I was 4 and it was the greatest experience of my life, from birthday parties to nap time. This place has really helped me grow as a human being, to have integrity and to have manners. I come from a family that isn't stable. So for them to take time out of their lives to help us is an amazing thing.

I remember as a child I would have an attitude and be mean to people. If I didn't get the things I wanted I would have a temper tantrum. By being a part of Sophia House I saw a whole different world. I feel privileged to be a part of Sophia House because there are a lot of people in the world that wish they had this much support. Sometimes I think, where would I be without Carol and Sophia House.

I remember going bowling, ice skating, to the beach, playing mancala, eating gold fish (crackers), celebrating Christmas, hiking, picnics, Chinese New Year, planting flowers, having art shows, playing an instrument, singing, swimming, gardening, origami, baking, painting, being with my best friend, naptime, lunchtime, snack time, the carnival, Easter and many more things.

Everyone at Sophia House has shaped me in some way. Ever since I was little, when people would help at Sophia House, I would learn that they went, or were going, to college. That was a big motivation for me.

Sophia House was my second home. They've helped me with my school, personal issues, and more. They helped me build up trust and valuable relationships. There was LOVE and people actually cared about the people they were with.

Pollie, high school junior
As of February 2017 Pollie is in her junior year of college.
She phones and visits frequently.

~

For most families that have been homeless, the same issues that led to their homelessness arise again in the first year or two of being housed. These issues include family and relationship problems, reuniting with an abusive partner, emotional instability, temporary unemployment, feelings of being overwhelmed, and being unable to meet the demands of life as a single mother with small children. Our close relationships with the families helped us know in advance when a situation was becoming critical and to help the mother take mitigating steps. It is very significant that all of our families were able to cope with problems as they arose without coming apart, having their children miss school, or becoming homeless again. They were able to build their inner and outer resources so they were no longer shattered when problems arose.

One of our mothers, Gail, lived in a van with her five children. Even under these extremely stressful conditions she managed to maintain a steady job at a charity store, where she first learned about Sophia Project. Soon she brought her three youngest children, ages one, two, and four to our daily programs. Shortly thereafter her name came up for a public housing unit. This provided her with a roof over her head but the conditions were difficult. The gang activity in front of her building forced her and her children to enter and leave the building through a side door in the basement.

Gail's own childhood was abusive and violent. She needed support to process her painful experiences. She had been to mental health counselors but none of them had been able to provide her with the safety and containment she needed to move through her trauma. Sophia Project helped Gail find an appropriate therapist and supported her in taking her medication regularly.

For several months Gail came to Sophia Project every day with her children. During that time we helped her reorient her life in several ways, including guidance in basic homemaking skills. Gail was already a great cook, so we helped her create a budget, maintain a cleaning and laundry schedule, and organize her household. Most of our focus was on storytelling, child development, and building parenting skills, including age-appropriate discipline.

Gail then started classes to prepare for her high school equivalency test. After passing her test she was offered a job as the teaching assistant for the GED prep class. Her two oldest children participated in the before-and-after-school program, the three younger children were in the early childhood or infant/toddler program. She wrote us this letter in 2005, after two years in the program.

Dear Sophia Project and Carol,

Thank you for all the support you have given my family during these past two years. Without your help I know I would still be in the situation that I found myself in. Your support has been a great help because I was given the chance to continue my education and obtain my GED. I only completed the ninth grade; therefore I am finally content with getting that part of my life closed. I am at ease knowing that I will continue my education and move on to college, which will enable me to provide a more stable life for my family. [My younger children] experience a "fairy tale" childhood under your care.

Thank you so much for all the ways you help my family. I feel you have provided us with proof that there is a different side to life. Thanking you for having a program like this is not enough to explain how grateful I am to have Sophia Project in my life. Everyone is so qualified, sweet, kind and lovable. You talk to my children and all the other children like they are delicate flowers; you treat them like they are so special to you. Thank you for providing everything that the children need from diapers and formula to clothes and birthday celebrations and all that wonderful care.

Thanks for having [my older children] in the program. I feel like this positive experience will provide them some type of stability in their lives. With the growing pain from their past they will learn to console and substitute them with what they learned from Sophia Project and everyone in it. I have faith that in time my effort and your support will heal [my child's] resentment problem. I am grateful that you set aside individual time for her.

Christmas has been great this year . . . Not only have you made my children happy but you have really financially helped me out. In no way had I experienced this nurturing love from anyone before; it is so unique in my personal and children's life.

Thank You

Gail attended community college and earned a certificate in medical record-keeping. She steadily advanced in the field and now fully supports her family. Her two older children are stable and content, and her three younger children are thriving; one is now on the honor roll at a private high school where she has earned a scholarship.

Assessment

Assessment was integral to our work. It was essential to assess the effectiveness of our methods by documenting outcomes for the children and families we served. Expertly assisted by Kay Sherman, we put a great deal of effort into designing an outcome measurement system to assess how well the children and mothers were progressing during and after their time in our daily programs. We developed a set of twelve child-development indicators and four parent-functioning indicators, which we used at specified points in the course of each family's program involvement. The twelve child development indicators are:

1. Physical development
2. Speech and language
3. Play
4. Social interaction
5. Psychological and emotional health
6. Safety, stability, and belonging
7. Connection to the natural world and to the arts and culture
8. Cognitive development
9. Resilience
10. Imagination
11. Kindergarten readiness
12. School performance

The four indicators of parent functioning are:

1. Housing status
2. Financial viability
3. Household stability, rhythm, and order
4. Child development practices

The most challenging family circumstance was when mental illness affected an adult in the household who had little contact with Sophia Project coworkers. The situation was less unstable when a mother was struggling with mental illness because she received adequate support through her daily contact with Sophia Project. Mental illness in the home produced environments that were volatile and unpredictable. This condition required constant ongoing support to keep the household stable. Consequently we limited the number of families with mental health issues participating in the program at any one time. We were able to work successfully with mothers diagnosed as mentally challenged or functioning at lower cognitive levels. We were best able to serve families who struggled with poverty, homelessness, isolation, and domestic violence.

Children not a part of the early childhood programs and struggling with issues of mental health or severely impaired emotional health needed many years of family support and therapeutic intervention, often experiencing several significant setbacks before being able to stabilize. Having received this support, they have all stabilized. In contrast, children in the early childhood program who were also struggling with mental or emotional health issues stabilized much more quickly and needed little or no therapeutic intervention after graduating from the early childhood program. These children are thriving.

To date (February 2017), we consistently find that children who were a part of the early childhood programs are socially and emotionally very well and are actively engaged in the world. Those children who were only a part of the before-and-after-school program are stable but sometimes lack the self-confidence and social skills of graduates of the early childhood program.

Part Two of this book includes the document, "Gauging the Effectiveness of Sophia Project," a complete description of the outcome measurement system we created in 2004-5. Part Two also includes a summary form of the child and parent indicators, with assessment and outcome stages.

~

I Think I Am Ready to Make a New Start
Sophia Project Newsletter 2004

Carolyn and her twin daughters have been intent upon transforming the chaos of their lives. This summer Carolyn found the strength and courage needed to end a longstanding emotionally abusive relationship. Then there was a fire in which their apartment burnt down. As we talked over the options, Carolyn said, " It is as if I am now fully awake. I can see what I can do, I feel a lot better about myself, the girls are happy and easy to take care of now, I know what to do with them. I think I am ready to make a new start. Do you think I can do it?" With the help of the Red Cross the family has moved into a better neighborhood. We stay in close contact. Carolyn has one good part time job and is looking for another. On our last phone conversation the girls told us they have been teaching their new friends the Sophia House games, like string games, drawing stories, and jump rope. "But," they add, "We better come to Sophia House for Halloween cause we can't do that by ourselves."

Other families stay in the neighborhood and make changes here, one step by courageous step. Having learned at Sophia House the importance of daily life, Joan now has a dinner table where most evenings she eats with her children. "The neighbors can't believe I am still doing it," she laughs. Some of her neighbor's children join her family for a sit-down dinner. "They'll be making their folks do it too one day" she smiles. Painfully this new order does not suit all of her extended family and some do not come around much anymore. "I miss them," she tells me, "but we have to do this now, the kids don't need to act like nothing matters." Other changes too have come about in her family, such as bedtime stories instead of falling asleep by the TV. Her four-year-old insists on an orderly environment if only around her own sleeping space. These may sound like small and insignificant changes but it is important to remember that they happen in extremely cramped quarters amid daily struggles with violence, poverty and depressingly overwhelming obstacles.

Our children and families are in a position to transform some of the most intractable problems of our society. As they become well they become agents of change within the harshness and chaos that created many of the problems.

Chapter Four:
Seeds for the Future

In 2008, its ninth year, Sophia Project was flourishing. All programs were operating at capacity. The children were thriving. All families remained housed. We had received an award for neighborhood renewal. Because the children and mothers remained healthy and stable, foundations were eager for other agencies to learn best practices from Sophia Project. Oakland Children's Hospital, Child Protective Services, and other social service agencies contacted us frequently, hoping to enroll their clients in Sophia Project programs. We had a successful coworker education program and a skilled, dedicated, and committed group of coworkers. We owned Sophia House outright and although the nationwide recession had an impact, our fundraising efforts were successful.

David and I had reached a point in our lives where we needed to transition to roles that did not require 24/7 availability. An earnest, ongoing, multi-pronged search for successors had not been successful. The search continued in 2009, still unsuccessful. We understood clearly that significant changes would be necessary if successors could not be found.

Our first priority was to protect the gains made by the 112 children and 48 families we served in our daily and followup programs. We had learned that once a child and family had joined Sophia Project their transformation from crisis and isolation to stability and community took at least five years, the first half in intensive daily programs and the second half in the family support program, through which services lessened in intensity over time.

At the end of the 2009 school year, two thirds of the children and families in the daily education programs were coming to the natural end of their time in those programs. In June 2010 the remaining third of the children and families would complete the daily program. They would then begin the three-year process of strengthening their gains and becoming gradually free from their need for assistance while participating in the family support program.

In 2009 we might have admitted new children and families to begin the next five- to six-year cycle, but it would have been irresponsible to take new children without experienced coworkers willing to commit to three years of intensive daily education programs followed by three years of support services.

When a family started in Sophia Project programs they began to let go of lifestyles and relationships that were not serving them well, including ad hoc childcare arrangements. Although these arrangements and relationships were far from ideal, most were better than no arrangements at all. Program closures needed to be done mindfully, ensuring that the needs of current children and families would be met. We resolved that we would admit new children only if the full amount of time needed for stabilization would be available. We would not risk closing programs when children and families were only midway through the stabilization process, as this could leave them without the necessary capacities to stabilize themselves and without their old systems of survival.

In 2008 we made a five-year plan that we would follow in the event successors were not found. As we were unable to find successors we followed this plan:

- 2008-9 school year: All programs continued in both houses.
- July 2009: Myrtle House was closed and sold, the proceeds funded the next school year's programs.
- 2009-10 school year: Sophia House provided program space for all remaining children in the daily programs. Before-and-after-school and respite programs continued. Formal intern training ended. Family support program continued to be developed and refined.
- July 2010: Sophia House was closed and sold. The proceeds funded the following years of family support.

As anticipated, by July 2010 all the children and families completed the intensive daily phase and graduated to the family support phase. Sophia Project transitioned from operating daily education programs and family support programs to a total focus on the family support program through which we continued parent education and the protection of children's healthy development.

In August 2010 Ellie Wood, a board member since the founding of Sophia Project, generously made available to the Sophia Project a house in San Rafael. The house was renovated to meet the needs of the Expanded Family Support Program that operated in 2010-13.

The Expanded Family Support Program included the following components:
- ***Serving as an Extended Family:*** This component continued to be an important part of every child's and every mother's relationship with Sophia Project. It included emergency and scheduled overnight respite care, individual meetings,

workshops, art and creative writing sessions, guidance, referrals, home visits, and emotional support, as well as outings and celebrations of important occasions in the lives of the children and families.

- **Rainy Day Assistance:** This component assisted families with occasional shortfalls, helping to cover utility, healthcare, or food bills, or the purchase of shoes or a school uniform.

- **Leap Forward:** Families continued to transition from homelessness to stability through program support. As they became ready to take the next steps, becoming more active members of their communities and ready to give back to the communities where they lived and worked, they sometimes required support for these steps. The Leap Forward component funded larger one-time costs that allowed the child or family to take a significant step forward. These costs included: housing security deposits, durable low-cost furniture for new stable housing, adult education opportunities, and assistance for improved treatment of chronic health issues.

- **Education Fund:** Tuition support through the Ellie Wood Education Fund for parochial school, essential school supplies, and college test and application fees.

- **Loan Fund:** This component allowed our families to access short-term no-interest loans for personal or family emergencies. Typical loans were approximately $300 and they were paid back within 3 to 6 months. The total loan fund was $5,000.

As a part of the Expanded Family Support program we offered workshops for the children and mothers. When mothers first joined Sophia Project, they were often unable to participate in classes and workshops because they felt ill at ease with themselves and/or unable to listen. After years of participating in the daily programs, mothers could more easily assimilate new information in a small workshop format. We provided or arranged for several workshop topics, including:

- Health screenings and check-ups for mothers and children.

- Nutritious food.

- Creating education and life goals.

- Getting organized and creating order in a chaotic world.

As the children grew older they required different forms of support. To meet the particular needs of middle school and high school children, we helped our parents identify their child's needs and then provided or directed the youth to workshops, which included:

- Public speaking, to help them feel comfortable speaking in a group setting
- Conflict prevention and resolution
- My word is my bond: the importance of thoughtfulness and trust
- Drug and alcohol awareness
- Sexuality

Our total focus on family support allowed us to anchor the children and families in their new communities and schools. Through the Expanded Family Support Program we worked with the families in ways not possible when we were running daily programs. These services included, for example, arranging for transportation to intensive six- to eight-week sessions on anger management, caring for the children of a mother who needed to be in the hospital for a month, working intensely with a child to overcome a learning disability, and offering more frequent respite care.

~

A Note from One of the Mothers
Sophia Project Newsletter, 2011

Things changed in my life. It seemed like suddenly, just as I had the bull by its horns, out of the blue, my life was turned around and I felt lost. I am grateful for the support of the last 6 years. Sophia Project is no longer doing daycare but they are still here in our lives. It was scary for a moment when Sophia Project said the daycare was closing. I thought, "I'm alone again."

It is hard to steer teenagers in the right direction when there are not good role models in their life. They look up and say, "No one cares and I can just do whatever I want." But I had help. When I thought my 15-year-old daughter was going to make a mistake, I made a plan for her and Sophia Project was there for me, encouraged me, and helped me financially.

My family is closer now. My teenage girls talk to me and they are so happy to be stable. My fifth-grade daughter tries to excel at all she does. My two younger children in elementary school are just wonderful. They know how to use their imaginations and to get along well with others. As for me, Sophia Project helped me reach the goals I made for myself. I did in four years what I thought would take me five. That included the setback of losing my brother to suicide.

I do want to share my experience with other people. Hitting a wall is not the end; the world does not stop there. Grounding yourself can be hard but it is so much worth it. Life is so beautiful and when I feel down I just lift my head up a little more, to see beyond the middle of the trees. I see and stare at a new vision that includes the tips of those trees, the mountain, and the different colors the world has to offer.

Thank you for making Sophia Project.

Success and Succession

As David and I recommended, the board voted to dissolve the Sophia Project 501(c)(3) effective in February 2014. With the gracious help of board member Patricia Kenney-Schliebe, work continued on an informal, personal basis for those children and families still needing support. In July 2014 we had our last big event, when former coworkers Martin and Jana and their two-year-old daughter visited California to celebrate their marriage with the children and families. It was a very happy reunion.

As this is being written in February 2017, we are in contact with many parents and children by mail or phone. Sometimes they call for consultation, but often they call just to make sure we are still here, to say hello, or to update us on a situation. Eight children continue to receive support through the Education Fund, seven children and four families still require respite care and weekly support. Those we see weekly are families with especially difficult circumstances, including parents with mental health issues, foster children who have aged out of the system, and single mothers with large families. We will accompany some of these children until they can be independent and stable, which for most should be only a few years in the future. As emergencies arise we are grateful we can provide emotional support, offer help negotiating life challenges in high school and college, and give short- or long-term respite care as long as it is needed.

Sophia Project is lasting proof that the Waldorf early childhood education and Camphill life-sharing models can address the needs of children and families who have experienced homelessness, trauma, and isolation. Sophia Project demonstrated that deep healing is possible through intensive services, a wise approach to education, and a thoughtful, caring live-in community. To summarize:

- Dozens of children and families participated in Sophia Project-sponsored neighborhood events and community festival celebrations.
- Fifty-five children received intensive therapeutic early childhood education and care, giving each one a chance to fulfill her or his potential and develop into a caring adult able to bring positive change to her or his community.
- Sophia House served another 57 children through respite care, art programs, and family support. These children received hope and joy, and have been recognized as unique and important. They too are doing remarkably well in their lives.

- As of February 2017, fifteen Sophia Project children are in college, and more are expected to enroll in the coming years. The college girls often say they will remember everything that they did in Sophia House so one day they can replicate it all with their own children.

- Forty-eight families at risk of recurring homelessness received family support services. They continue to be housed and stable, in many instances bringing that stability to their new communities. No Sophia Project family has ever returned to homelessness.

- Except for those with mental health issues, the mothers are all working. Many are also in adult training programs or in school.

- Thirty-five interns and coworkers were trained at Sophia House; many continue to work with vulnerable children.

- Sophia Project helped establish three new communities of service: Thamurai in India (by providing consultation and training); Mariposa in Rhode Island (by providing consultation and funding); and The Community School for Creative Education in Oakland (by providing consultation and assisting with community meetings through presentations, demonstrations, and childcare).

- Two neighborhood homes were improved and beautified and are now occupied by civic-minded extended families.

Despite our best efforts to solve the succession problem, we were unable to do so. The long hours, intense work, and low pay accounted for some of the difficulty. And yet, many Waldorf teachers and Camphill coworkers work long hours doing intense work for little pay. The prospect of working in difficult inner-city neighborhoods deterred some people. It was important for Sophia Project to offer high-quality early childhood education, family support, and the example of a nonviolent, life-affirming community right in the neighborhood where many of our families lived. The mothers and children often told us that it was very important that Sophia Project existed in their own community, not only because it uplifted the neighborhood (the children often proudly said they lived just down the street from Sophia House) but also because it made the practices seem more accessible. The mothers felt that it was within their grasp to replicate in their own homes much of what they experienced at Sophia Project.

The crime and violence of the neighborhood did not directly enter our homes. An important reason for this is the kind of work we were doing. It has repeatedly been my experience, both here and in other countries, that good quality early childhood work creates islands of peace. This is because young children are still in the universally human stage of development. All infants need protection and warmth to develop and grow healthily. In the first year of life children everywhere are learning to stand, in the second year children everywhere are learning to talk. Similarly, in every culture, three-, four-, and five-year-old children have the same developmental stages. Most people understand this and can, despite disagreement in other aspects of life, agree upon the needs of

the very young child. This shared humanity has often been the starting point for finding common ground and bringing about positive social change.

Several prospective coworkers cited insecurity of future work and isolation as deterrents for joining the work. To some extent this is an unavoidable experience when serving families who lack basic security in the world and who experience debilitating isolation. However, coworker isolation could perhaps be mitigated.

Sophia Project received invaluable support from many individual members of the Anthroposophical Society, Waldorf teachers and parents, members of the Christian Community, and Camphill coworkers. Without this network of spiritual, emotional, academic, and financial support, Sophia Project would surely not have been successful. As a Camphill affiliate we received critical support especially in the area of intern recruitment and immigration. As an organization, however, we never managed to be a fully recognized member of Camphill or WECAN. The reasons for this were mostly related to organizational bylaws and regulations. Regrettably, for some prospective coworkers the lack of full recognition amplified the feeing of isolation and played a part in their hesitation to join us.

If future endeavors like Sophia Project could be formally linked to a Camphill or Waldorf organization, prospective teachers and coworkers could join the project with greater confidence. Such an affiliation would also support and enhance coworker education.

An Urgent Need

Sophia Project Newsletter, 2009

It is a gift to witness the wisdom the young child embodies, as seen in the following story about one of our four-year-olds.

Sarah has endured many hardships including living in a car for nearly a year with her mother and four siblings and the toxic levels of chaos and stress those circumstances produce. On a recent morning Sarah placed several stuffed animals in a semicircle on the floor in front of her. She tenderly looked at them all. Then, looking at one older dog whose head flops due to many years of being carried around by his neck, she said, "This one is poor. I love all of them but I'm gonna love this one more, then he won't be poor."

Sarah knows what is needed to bring healing to both outer and inner poverty. At some level she knows that those who have been damaged can be healed by love.

The connection between a nurturing early childhood education and success in later life is clear. As inequalities become more savage in the current political and cultural climate, the urgent needs of urban young children are alarming. The 2015 Save The Children report, "The Urban Disadvantage," states:

> Save the Children examined infant mortality in capital cities of wealthy (OECD) countries and found that Washington, DC had by far the highest infant mortality rate among the 25 capital cities.
>
> ". . . . urban neighborhoods with high poverty rates often have much higher infant mortality rates than the city average, and Save the Children found that city averages often mask the huge disparities in infant death rates between rich and poor children. In 2012, for example, infants in Washington, DC's Ward 8, where half of all children live in poverty, died at a rate more than 10 times higher than the death rate of infants born in Ward 3, the richest part of the city."[1]

Many people long for community but do not know how to build one. In addition to meeting urgent needs, living examples of functioning communities can greatly assist young people who are searching for meaning and a sense of belonging to find or create positive alternatives to destructive elements in society.

Seeds for the Future

Many former Sophia Project coworkers continue to work serving vulnerable children. The coworkers and children who brought Sophia Project to life now carry its seeds into the future, so it is fitting to end this account with their words.

The following excerpts by former coworkers originally appeared in the 2013 Sophia Project Newsletter. Excerpts by teenagers appeared in the Newsletter in 2012.

I was first introduced to the nonprofit circuit through AmeriCorps working for the Sophia Project, an organization that supported vulnerable families within disadvantaged, low-income communities. I worked and lived among the most remarkable people who exemplified what it means to be empathetic and socially responsible. The work itself was simultaneously discouraging because of the need and inspiring because of the change. All the families the Project served were on the road to recovery from homelessness, and with the Sophia

Project as a support and guide that path was promising for each family. The Sophia Project encompassed the power of community, the impact of kindness and the sincerest form of compassion. The Sophia Project opened my world and changed the course of "what I want to be when I grow up." Since my time with the Project I have sought out non-profit work, I am currently working for a philanthropic organization that invests in fighting poverty in the Bay Area. I was attracted to this organization as the core principles align closely with the values I learned at Sophia Project, namely, that each person deserves a fair shot at a good education, attentive healthcare, safe housing, and dependable employment. The Project changed the course of so many lives for the better, it changed the course of my life as well. I truly feel humbled and grateful for my time with the Sophia Project.

Sophie Jaggi

When I was called to share my experiences with Sophia Project I found myself torn about what to say. Should I mention that I think of my service life in terms of before and after Sophia Project, that I was shown a whole new level of depth in understanding, honoring and meeting the needs of others? Alternately, do I describe how I witnessed the innocent and hopeful light inside of the children gently and carefully preserved by the safety, consistency and attentiveness in the houses, even when life circumstances threatened to dim that light? Or tell of the day when the drug dealers outside one of the houses offered to help us in our effort to sweep the broken glass and syringe needles that littered the sidewalk each night? Ultimately, I admit that my experience at Sophia Project had, and has continued to have, an effect on me and my life in service that is as profound and far-reaching as it is difficult to describe in brief. As a counselor I look forward to applying this depth of compassion to those that I serve, such that I can continue in this critical and sensitive work of healing with gentle, loving attentiveness. More than anything, from the living examples of Carol, David and my fellow coworkers, I walked away from the project with the unshakeable conviction that as dark as life may seem at times, loving, dedicated service can truly transform even the bleakest darkness into light.

Derek Rugsaken, counselor

Living and working at Sophia Project was an enriching and nourishing experience that has inspired me and influenced my relationships and attitude towards myself and others, especially babies and young children. It is a life long lesson and I will always feel privileged and thankful that I could be part of the extended family Sophia Project is for so many children and families. Martin and I have settled now in Camphill in Scotland where we work with young adults with additional support needs. Martin and I both feel that one day we will carry the Sophia Project impulse on and create a healing, nourishing and loving home for those who need it. We would strive to apply all that we have learned from Carol and David.

Jana Pazourkova (now Alfred), Camphill Cairnlee

I have been honored and very fortunate to be a part of Sophia Project. Sophia Project has shown me that a group of like-minded people can come together and make a real difference in people's lives. This experience has also taught me that it's not just about providing necessities (food, shelter, clothing, education, etc.) and finding resources for those who need it. It's also about providing warmth, stability, and a sense of belonging by becoming part of their lives and developing a supportive relationship. I have learned that many small differences can make a HUGE difference. I am amazed by the resiliency these families have developed and that they are able to transform their lives and overcome their obstacles to living a better life. Throughout my career, I will carry Sophia Project values with me and remember that it is a way of being that can help make a difference.

Tracy Weber
social worker serving mothers and children from birth
to three in a residential substance abuse program

Returning from the Peace Corps with a budding interest in early childhood education, I joined Sophia Project. There in West Oakland, providing child care and support to families stabilizing after homelessness and other crises, I witnessed a miracle. I saw mothers complete a GED or job training, find work, begin to smile as they discovered a new image of themselves. I saw children come alive again after abuse, turn destructive anger into creativity, delve deeply into the imaginative play that will one day become their adult capacity for aspiration and goal setting. Sophia Project is winding up as an organization, but having witnessed success, I aspire to provide this quality of care to vulnerable families.

Windsong Bergman
teacher, Early Head Start special needs

Sophia Project encapsulated everything I was looking for at age 25. A Camphill community, Waldorf education, and work with vulnerable children and families. I felt enormously honored to have had the privilege of working there and felt humbled by their courage and strength to overcome adversity. All in all I was there for 5 years and in those years witnessed such extraordinary positive transformation in both the children and mothers that I was often brought to tears.

There are many things that I have learnt during my time at Sophia Project but there are perhaps two things that stand out for me. The one is that if you truly want to make a difference in a child or family's life you need to be "in it for the long haul." That means years of work helping them through all the ups and downs until the obstacles lessen and life is more stable. The other thing that stands out for me is this: I feel that the children I have worked with in my time at Sophia Project have showed me that through providing love, understanding and a safe place to be a child they can, through their extraordinary capacities, heal the wounds of abuse. This gives me hope and for that I am eternally grateful.

Anna Sands
founding kindergarten teacher in an urban, state Steiner school, United Kingdom

I have carried with me the impulse of Sophia Project in all the work I have done since leaving the project. Much of my work has been within governmental agencies or those funded in part by government: Community Mental Health, Child Protective Services (CPS) and now Early Intervention with children, birth to three, who have developmental delays or disabilities. Within these systems, there is little patience or time for the slow, intentional and individualized work that was so much a part of the healing and transformation that took place within mothers and children at Sophia Project. Although this is frustrating and, at times, deeply saddening, I approached this obstacle with the belief that small moments of healing and wonder, and small acts of kindness and compassion do matter. In my CPS work with the mothers who had abused or neglected their children, I always take care to treat them with the dignity I know they possess as human beings. With the children who waited in the CPS office to be taken to foster homes we found a box and made a "house," a safe place for them to play while they waited. In my work now, I show some mothers how to play with their children, how to get on the floor and join their child and see the world from their view. With many mothers, I emphasize the importance of rhythm, especially for those children who have experienced the trauma of homelessness, domestic violence and the effects of substance abuse. Sophia Project taught me to recognize these moments, however small or fleeting, of healing, teaching, learning and transformation.

Sarah Deurloo

Finally, the words of two teenagers whom we served at Sophia House:

I remember coming over to Sophia House every Tuesday to spend the night. It would be just me and Sophie (an intern) and we would do homework, eat dinner, play games, talk, and maybe even watch movies. Every Tuesday was a special day. It was a day to relax. I remember coming every day in the morning and Carol or Martin or even Tracy (who was usually busy with the infants) would check our homework or let us finish what needed to be done. We would have breakfast, then off to school.

Sophia House has changed me in so many ways. Sophia House was like a second home. They all cared for me, showed love. They always pushed me for the better. They always made sure I was doing good and always doing my best. Thanks to Carol, I'm the person I am today, meaning I'm always trying my best in everything I do. I never give up and I'm always thinking positive. Sophia House is a place you can count on. They never give up on you even though you try to give up, they just won't let you. Sophia House is a loving, caring, amazing place to be. No one could ever regret this place. It is a place you can call home. Sophia House has been there since my baby brother and sister were babies. They taught them everything they needed to know and even prepared them for school. When I am sad or down I still come to the people here.

Sophia House is a place I know I can always come to.

Julia
Julia experienced a harrowing childhood but is now successfully working as an administrative assistant, attending college, and engaged in a healthy social life.

When I think of Sophia House, I remember the warm loving memories growing up as a child. Sophia House has always been a place I felt loved and safe, and I always had fun. It was here where I first learned to knit; to this day I continue to enjoy this activity. I love being creative and Sophia House was where I could express myself. The friendships I've made at Sophia House are priceless. I met two of my closest friends here. One I happen to go to school with. Sophia House will always be a part of who I am. It will always be in my heart. I could never forget this place and the sweet memories I made being a part of here. It means that much to me. Sometimes I wish I were a child again so I could relive the time I spent here at Sophia House.

This is my inspiration, to give back to people, to my community, children, and people who have been through similar situations as me. To teach people what I've learned, to inspire someone to do something they love or to give a helping hand. This is what I want to do in my future. My inspiration came from Sophia House and the people here that love me so much.

Cherie

Endnotes

1. Save the Children, "The Urban Disadvantage," 41-42. *Save the Children Resource Center* (2015). resourcecentre.savethechildren.net/node/9052/pdf/sowm_2015.pdf.

Nourishing and protecting the light within each child

Part Two

Documents

Gauging the Effectiveness of Sophia Project

Goal setting, observation, record keeping, and systematic evaluation were integral to the work with the children, mothers, and coworkers. In 2004-5 Kay Sherman and I developed an outcome measurement system. Some funders requested an accompanying narrative describing the development of the system. In response to this request we created the document "Gauging the Effectiveness of Sophia Project," which is reproduced here in its original unedited form.

Sophia Project has continually refined and articulated what we do and why we do it for the families we serve, centering our purpose around healing the damage to children's cognitive, social, and emotional development that is typically caused by the chaos and deprivation of homelessness and poverty-driven unstable living arrangements. Through our ongoing relationships and observations we know that to date all of the children who have "graduated" from our early childhood program are participating well in school and all of our families remain housed and stable.

Sophia Project has acquired enough experience about our purposes and methods to design an outcome measurement system that ties the needs of incoming children and their families to the Project's program methods and ultimately to changes in the health and well-being of the children and their families. The resulting outcome measures for individual children and their families are intended to help Sophia Project answer questions about how effective we have been in helping the children served to date, and whether there are identifiable groups of children that are helped more or less by the services that Sophia Project provides.

The Sophia Project Model

Sophia Project offers daily programs for children ranging from infants to school-age based on the best child development practices. However, the project serves children and families with extraordinary needs. Our goal is to reverse – or at least alleviate to some degree – the developmental delays and the extreme emotional fragility of children that typically result from their parents' stressful experiences of being homeless, in deep poverty, without the financial security, information and other resources to create consistent, healthy environments for their children to grow and learn.

The families Sophia Project serves are typically headed by a young single mother who is experiencing high and sustained levels of stress and struggling to stabilize.

Typically she is unable to meet the needs of her young children. It may take several years for her to gain the capacities needed to nurture her children and stabilize the family. It is critical that the needs of the young children are met during this time in order to give them the best possible chance of success in school and later in life.

While we support parents intensively and in many ways, especially helping them improve their child development practices, our primary focus is on the children, for three main reasons: 1) More than two decades of research on programs and policies designed to help disadvantaged parents indicates that even when these efforts are successful the benefits do not necessarily "trickle down"[1] to children. 2) Current education theorists recognize a phenomenon of cumulative deficits that children from disadvantaged families build over their preschool years and subsequent school careers resulting in a persistent and substantial gap between the outcomes of poor children and those raised in middle-class homes that is not explained solely by monetary resources, but which may be effectively addressed outside the children's homes.[2] 3) Research on resiliency in children – i.e., their capacity to overcome adverse circumstances – indicates that the availability of strong, supportive, and consistent attention from other adults in their lives (i.e., outside their immediate families) is often the key to success.[3]

Sophia Project is sometimes referred to by funders as "therapeutic child care," which emphasizes the healing aspect of our work with children who have been traumatized or whose development has been interrupted by very difficult life circumstances. We refer to ourselves as a "child development center," which emphasizes the normal unfolding of children's capacities in a favorable environment. Whichever label is used, the work with children and their parents is based, in part, on these principles:

- Predictable daily activities and familiar people in their environment help children gain a sense of control and security. Sophia Project staff strives to create a calming rhythm to the daily experiences of children and parents and to promote familiarity by "assigning" staff to be responsible for meeting the needs of the same children from day to day.

- Children's success in learning new responses and behaviors requires consistency in signals from adults, a lot of repetition, and praise. Sophia Project staff strives to create a culture of considerate social interaction by modeling it among themselves and between themselves and the children and parents, and by reinforcing it for the children's interactions with each other. In addition, the staff's usual form of correcting children's behavior is to say something similar to, "We don't do that here," so as not to set up a moral judgment about how things might be done at home.

- An emotional "even keel," the brain work of learning, and physical growth are supported by good nutrition. Sophia Project serves healthy meals and snacks every day, minimizing sugar, and incorporating organically grown foods, and foods from our own gardens when possible.

- Cognitive development in children, in addition to being founded in good physical and emotional health, requires education for all the senses, a variety of experiences, and an emphasis on play as the principal method for learning in young children. Sophia Project incorporates many standard early childhood education activities and approaches in its daily work with children, but relies most on the Waldorf early childhood education curriculum for the 3-5 year olds and intentionally excludes the "passive" forms of cognitive input–TV, videos, recorded music, etc.

- Children with major developmental issues, life experience traumas, and/or class disadvantages need "opportunity passports" to succeed in school. With this in mind, Sophia Project staff strive to ensure that children in its programs have all the zoo-visiting, arts and culture, and "wider-world exposure" experiences that their more advantaged age-peers are likely to have, as well as the cognitive/ language processing of these experiences that enable the children to share them effectively in their schools.

Sophia Project accepts children and families who have major challenges but whose parents have moved out of homeless shelters and have made some efforts to create stability for their children, and have expressed a clear commitment to work with Sophia Project staff to create more stability and opportunities for their children. Programs include an infant and toddler program based in Myrtle House for children from birth up to age 3; an early childhood education center in Sophia House for children from age three up to age 5; a before-and-after-school program for a few children whose siblings remain in the early childhood programs; and a weekend respite care program currently in both facilities serving the children and families who have left daily programs. All services are provided free of charge to parents and children and are supported by the fundraising efforts of Sophia Project.

For the purpose of assessment Sophia Project thinks about its program involvement with children and families in terms of four phases, from very intensive involvement to lessening involvement over time. Phase 1 is defined as participation of children in daily programs; in Phase 2, children are no longer involved in daily programs – usually because they have entered kindergarten or parents are able to provide other daily child care arrangements – but children and their parents are still connected by their frequent participation in Sophia Project events, individual celebrations for them, and other services as special needs arise, such as help purchasing extras for children's education, or acting as intermediary with schools and health agencies. In Phase 3 children and families still participate in special events and other services as special needs arise.

Sophia Project Compared to Other Early Childhood Education/Child Care Models
Early childhood education has been extensively evaluated to determine its benefits for children's development, school readiness and, for disadvantaged children, its long-term effect on life outcomes. Various child care arrangements for young children under age three have been extensively evaluated as well, focusing on differences between group child care models, family child care models, and individual substitute (for mothers) caregivers. In general, the quality of care in terms of its developmental focus has been an issue. Only the most intensive (and expensive) models have been shown to have effects on children's outcomes in the short and long term, but the measured effects of the most intensive interventions are substantial.[4] Because of this extensive history of evaluation, Sophia Project does not intend to prove the value of early childhood education for disadvantaged children as a general proposition. Rather, the challenge for Sophia Project is to document the effectiveness or *our* methods, based on the outcomes for the children and families *we* serve.

The first benchmark we consider for the effectiveness of our methods is that, compared to the early childhood intervention and education programs that have been evaluated, Sophia Project's daily programs for children up to age 6 are clearly both comprehensive and intensive. On average, children not yet in school are at Sophia House or Myrtle House five days a week for 9-12 hours per day with the full range of age-appropriate activities in groups and one-to-one, including indoor and outdoor play, education, music and art activities, meals, snacks, naps, hygiene, and special events, field trips and other outside activities. The programs also arrange for and provide transportation to health care, special-needs assessments and treatments, and other child services when parents are not able to manage these alone. For the 25 children currently (2005) served in daily programs, Sophia Project has ten full-time staff, including two certified Waldorf education teachers, one for each group – a child to staff ratio of 2.7 to 1, which is intensive by any standard. This same staff provides all direct services in all programs.

Beyond the time children spend with us and the number of staff we have available to work with them, we intend with our new outcome measurement system to gauge the quality of staff interactions with children and parents by assessing changes in the children's development and parents' functioning.

Outcome Measurement System

To assess how well the children and parents served by Sophia Project are progressing during and after their time in our daily programs, we have developed a set of 12 child indicators of development and four parent indicators of functioning which are used in a system of assessment at specified points in the history of families' program involvement. The assessments conducted at the first three points of measurement in this system enable Sophia Project to learn about the children and parents, especially their issues and needs. The assessments at the next three points of measurement are designed to reveal how well the program is working for the children and parents – i.e., their "outcomes." These points of measurement include:

- When families are accepted into Sophia Project – the "baseline" or "intake" point when initial impressions are gathered;

- After about two months of participation – a time for a closer look at emerging issues and needs;

- After about four months of participation – a time for a comprehensive assessment of issues and needs and a look at whether the daily rhythm of program activities seems to be having the intended calming and healing effect on children;

- After 18 months of participation – an early look at outcomes when adjustments in methods are possible;

- At the end of Phase 1, usually after about three years of daily program participation, when families move out of daily programs;

- At the end of Phase 2, when families' active involvement in events, respite care, and special needs services tails off and Sophia Project staff have a clear picture of what has changed for children and parents since the beginning of their involvement.

Our experience suggests that we learn most, but not everything, that is important to know at the first two assessment points. Then, at about four months into service programs, we are able to see whether the calming and healing effects of our program are "taking" and, if not, whether there may be underlying issues – neurological, medical, etc. – that require extra diagnostic help. This is the point at which we are particularly alert to special needs. The last measurement point – at the end of Phase 2 participation – is not necessarily the end of our relationship with children and their families, but it is the point at which we will make a judgment about whether children are on track developmentally and whether our intervention has been wholly or partially successful, or not successful, and the reasons for these outcomes.

For the most part, data for these indicators is gathered through observation of children and parents in day-to-day interactions rather than formal testing, although the child indicators are consistent with formal child development assessments based on observation instruments developed by the High Scope Educational Research Foundation, a 40+-year-old leader in the evaluation of early childhood education programs.[5]

The four indicators designed to evaluate the parents outcome include: (1) adequate family housing, (2) financial viability, (3) household stability, rhythm, and order, and (4) child development practices.

The indicators for children are: (1) physical development, (2) speech and language skills, (3) cognitive development, (4) psychological and emotional health, (5) social interaction, (6) play, (7) imagination, (8) resilience, (9) sense of belonging, (10) relationship to nature and the arts, (11) kindergarten readiness (for our 5-year-olds), and (12) school adjustment and achievement.

Presented in this way, the 12 child indicators might seem to be of equal importance. But, in fact, a few are "foundational" – meaning that without adequate development and/or stability in a few areas, progress and stability in other areas of child growth is blocked or made more difficult. Dr. T. Berry Brazelton describes this foundational nature of some aspects of child development as "the irreducible needs of children."[6] With Dr. Stanley I. Greenspan, he identifies five such child-oriented needs:

1.   Ongoing nurturing relationships, where nurturing particularly means adults who respond to children's signals of need, explorations, and achievements – because emotion precedes cognition;

2. Physical protection, safety and regulation, including protection from toxic substances and chaotic environments, and regulation of exposure to passive forms of cognitive input;

3. Experiences tailored to individual differences – i.e., recognizing and "nurturing a child's nature";

4. Developmentally appropriate experiences to help children master essential skills of self-control, interaction with people in their environment, emotional expression, imagination, thinking, and self-identity; and

5. Limit setting, structure and expectations with external rewards and methods to help children internalize controls on their behavior.[7]

The phenomenon of "foundational" experiences or "irreducible needs" accounts for some of the repetition in the indicators and suggests a complex, interactive relationship among the indicators. For example, children's feelings of safety, stability and belonging need to be addressed in order to promote their psychological and emotional health, and thus enable their cognitive development and positive social interactions. Other kinds of interactions must also be taken into account. For example, we have found that we must often return to examining the circumstances underlying indicators of physical development and speech and language development in order to assess how children's development in other areas is (or is not) progressing. We cannot expect children to respond optimally to the healing aspects of our daily programs if they have brain damage or neurological conditions that distort perception or inhibit learning. Thus, we work on all 12 child indicators at once, recognizing that the indicators of development are interrelated.

~

Reproduced on the following pages is the recording/assessment form used when a child first arrives at Sophia Project. In addition to individual recording forms, we created a summary recording form of the child and parent indicators – assessment and outcomes (see "Sophia Project Child Development and Parent Functioning Indicator System").

Sophia Project

BASELINE CHILD INDICATORS

Complete this form within 2 weeks of a family's acceptance into the Sophia Project. Complete separate Indicators form for each child in Sophia Project programs. Circle Yes or No and write descriptions where requested below.

Today's date: _____

Child name and age: _____

Parent name/s: _____

Names and ages of siblings in Sophia Project programs: _____

_____

_____

_____

1. Physical Development
Are growth, motor skills, hand-eye coordination and sensory integration on track for the child's age? *(circle one)* [YES] [NO]

If No, describe current limitations and potential problems, and any special methods needed to aid the child's development: _____

_____

_____

2. Speech and Language
Are the child's use of language, clarity of speech, and willingness to communicate verbally on track for his/her age? *(circle one)* [YES] [NO]

If No, describe current limitations and potential problems, and any special methods needed to aid development: _____

_____

_____

What languages does the child hear and use – home, school and elsewhere? _____

3. Cognitive Development

Through language, play, and adjustment to the Sophia Project rhythm (and learning through direct instruction, if applicable), does the child show age-appropriate cognitive development? (circle one) [YES]   [NO]

If No, describe current limitations and any special methods needed to aid development: _____

_____

4. Psychological and Emotional Health

Does the child respond to change, frustration, surprises, and other potential sources of upset in age-appropriate ways? Does s/he respond appropriately to warmth and interest? (circle one) [YES]   [NO]

If No, describe extreme responses – especially, withdrawn/depressed; continuous crying; hyperactive; or enraged/angry. Describe any special methods needed to aid calming, tolerance and/or engagement: _____

_____

5. Safety, Stability and Belonging

Does the child show confidence in his/her place in the world, attachment to particular people, places and things, and an appropriate level of fearfulness for his/her age and specific situations? (circle one) [YES]   [NO]

If No, describe areas of disturbance, behaviors, and any special methods needed to increase feelings of safety, stability and belonging. (Cross check with Parent Indicators.): _____

_____

_____

6. Social Interaction

Does the child relate to family members, other children, and caregivers/teachers in age-appropriate ways? (circle one) [YES]   [NO]

If No, describe areas of disturbance (family, peers, etc.), behaviors, and any special methods needed to help relationships develop: _____

_____

7. Play
Does the child engage objects in play, play alone, play with other children and caregivers/ teachers in age-appropriate ways? *(circle one)* [YES]   [NO]

If No, describe current limitations and potential problems, and any special methods needed to aid development: _____

_____

8. Imagination
Does the child demonstrate imaginative capacity and/or engage in fantasy play in age-appropriate ways? *(circle one)* [YES]   [NO]

If No, describe current limitations: _____

_____

9. Resilience
Does the child's functioning relative to the traumas of his/her early life and/or current circumstances show abilities for self-protection, problem-solving, hardiness (the ability to bounce back from adversity), and self-management? Is the child able to separate who s/he is from what is happening or has happened in her life circumstances – i.e., not internalize external conditions? *(circle one)* [YES]   [NO]

If Yes, describe areas of functioning that are stronger and weaker: _____

_____

10. Connection to the Natural World and to Arts and Culture
Does the child's history include any special connection to or experience with the natural world – positive or negative? *(circle one)* [YES]   [NO]

If Yes, describe special connection or experiences: _____

_____

Has the child had age-appropriate and mainstream experiences of the arts and culture? *(circle one)* [YES]   [NO]

If Yes, describe experiences: _____

_____

11. Kindergarten Readiness (only for children age 4 by September)

Is the child on track ready to have a successful kindergarten experience next year based on his/her cognitive, social, and emotional development? *(circle one)* [YES]   [NO]

If No, describe initially presenting issues that will need attention. (Cross check indicators 1, 2, 3, 4 and 6 above.): _____

_____

12. School Adjustment and Achievement (children age 6+)

Is the child's adjustment to school routines and expectations, and his/her achievement, in the normal range based on school report cards and/or conversation with teachers? *(circle one)* [YES]   [NO]

If No, describe issues that will need attention: _____

_____

SUMMARY OF BASELINE INDICATORS

How many "Yes" answers are circled above? _____

How many "No" answers? _____

What are the most important special needs of this child – beyond what the Sophia Project attempts to provide for every child in our programs? _____

_____

_____

_____

Endnotes

1   The research evidence from a variety of welfare reform programs operated in the 1990's – including those that provided relatively generous income and child care supports while encouraging welfare parents to go to work – reveal a mixed set of effects on children. See, for example, Pamela A. Morris, Lisa A. Gennetian, and Greg J. Duncan, "Effects of Welfare and Employment Policies on Young Children: New Findings on Policy Experiments conducted in the Early 1990's," *Social Policy Report*, Volume XIX, No. 2, 2005 (available at www.mdrc. org/NextGeneration). An earlier generation of programs aimed specifically at improving the outcomes, including kindergarten readiness, of low-income children by working with parents in home visitation models generally were found to have few of the intended effects. See, for example, "Home Visiting: Recent Program Evaluations," *The Future of Children*, 1999, Volume 9, No. 1 – available at www.futureofchildren.org.

2   The research on this phenomenon is discussed in the context of school reforms in Paul Tough, "What It Takes to Make a Student," *New York Times Magazine*, December 26, 2006 (p. 44).

3   See, for example, Emmy E. Werner and Ruth S. Smith, *Journeys From Childhood to Midlife: Risk, Resilience and Recovery* (Ithaca, NY: Cornell University Press, 2001).

4   See W. Steven Barnett and Clive R. Belfield, "Early Child Development and Social Mobility," in *The Future of Children: Opportunity in America*, Volume 16, Number 2 (Fall 2006), Woodrow Wilson School of Public and International Affairs at Princeton University and the Brookings Institution (www.futureofchildren.org).

5   See High/Scope Educational Research Foundation, Preschool Child Observation Record, 2nd Edition, and Child Observation Record for Infants and Toddlers, described and available for order at www.highscope.org.

6   T. Berry Brazelton, M.D. and Stanley I. Greenspan, M.D., *The Irreducible Needs of Children: What Every Child Must Have to Grow, Learn, and Flourish* (Cambridge, MA: DeCapo Press, 2000).

7   Brazelton and Greenspan also identify two needs of children that must be met in the wider world of policy and politics: Stable, supportive communities and cultural continuity that provide parallel benefits for parents, groups, and neighborhoods to those that children need in their development – e.g., connection, identity, skills, opportunities, empowerment; and policies to assure the future of children that provide the "security of having physical needs met," foster "ongoing human relationships that preserve and support families and communities," and support "families, educational settings and communities that help children become communicative, reflective members of society."

Funding and Volunteers

None of our work with children and mothers would have been possible without the support of our donors—individuals, foundations, and corporations. A great many hours were spent on publicity and fundraising. Below is a very brief synopsis of this aspect of our work.

Sophia Project was blessed with outstanding volunteers. Chief among them were the members of our board of trustees. Ably led by Robert McDermott, and for one important year skillfully led by Patricia Kenney-Schliebe, the board held as a central responsibility the protection of the programs serving the children and mothers. In addition to providing generous financial support, board members devoted many hours to legal and fiduciary oversight, fundraising, and public events. Several board members also worked in our programs with the children.

In its financial oversight the board had the advantage of excellent financial reports provided by David Barlow. Board members, some of whom were involved with financial institutions, consistently remarked upon the transparent, precise, and comprehensive quality of the reports.

The Sophia Project was financed through fundraising; our families were unable to pay for our services. Sophia Project did not receive government funding; 65 percent of our budget came from foundations, 34 percent from individuals, and 1 percent directly from corporations. Many individual donors were associated with the Anthroposophical Society, Waldorf education, or Camphill, but less than 2 percent of funds came from Camphill or other anthroposophical institutions.

Sophia Project had two large fundraising events. At the outset, those of us who planned the events agreed that it would be contradictory to raise funds for children who were often hungry and mothers who had been the victims of alcohol-fueled domestic violence at an event that had the potential to waste large quantities of food or encourage over indulgence in alcohol. We settled on an "elegant evening of art, music, and good company." World-famous opera star and Sophia Project board member Frederica von Stade thrilled guests with wonderful performances. Artists from the Association of Clay and Glass Artists of California exhibited and sold their juried, beautiful works of ceramic and glass. We raised slightly over $100,000 at each of these events and of course gained new individual donors.

Individual donors also came to Sophia Project through house parties given by board members, and talks given in various venues. Our newsletters and flyers always contained drawings of the houses and children but, in consultation with the families served by Sophia Project, no photographs of the children or families. As one mother put it, "When we were homeless it was not important but now we are almost getting normal and we will just be a part of the neighborhood, so if you don't have to . . . " To ensure that children and families continued to feel the Sophia Houses were safe places to heal and grow without risk of shame or exposure to the larger community, then or in future years, we were happy to honor their request.

Sophia Project fit into the granting guidelines of the majority of the foundations that gave core support over many years. We also received grants from foundations whose general guidelines we did not fit. Some notable examples include the California Endowment, the Cowell Foundation, and the Barbro Osher Pro Suecia Foundation.

The California Endowment is concerned primarily with physical health. Because they valued our work, the concept of health was expanded in our case to include general well-being. Similarly, Sophia Project was outside the geographic guidelines of the Cowell Foundation but the foundation made an exception in our case because it wished to show support for the kind of work we were doing. The Barbro Osher Pro Suecia Foundation provides support to nonprofit organizations that benefit Swedish education, culture, and arts. The foundation granted Sophia Project funds because they were impressed with the quality of care for the children and the simple, practical beauty of the houses. On one occasion Barbro Osher invited Princess Madeleine of Sweden to visit Sophia House. The Princess (and her bodyguards) very kindly visited on a day that happened to be one of the children's birthday. That child received a special present, a real princess sang happy birthday to her, in Swedish and in English.

The Academy for the Love of Learning, based in Santa Fe, New Mexico, granted funds to Sophia Project for the parenting education program. The values of Sophia Project aligned with those of the Academy, which was at the time exploring the field of parenting work with an eye to beginning that work in Santa Fe. As an adjunct faculty of the Academy, I developed the Sophia Project parenting program and then reported on this work at meetings of the Academy board of trustees.

Sophia Project also received support from several organizations, notably the Omidyar Network, that do not accept proposals but contact projects they wish to support.

Every year we successfully funded our proposed budget. All our written proposals and formal presentations stated that our work was informed by Steiner/Waldorf education principles and König/Camphill community principles. Our proposals stated that, based on our principles, we had developed a program that effectively:

- Supported the healing and normal development of young traumatized children through a curriculum of early intervention, early childhood education, before-and-after-school care, and weekend respite care all designed to meet these children's specific needs.

- Provided parents struggling with poverty, toxic levels of stress, homelessness, and domestic violence with parenting education, no-fee full-time therapeutic care with 24/7 availability as needed, and family support programs crafted to meet the needs of each individual family.

- Helped to revitalize the low-income neighborhood in which the two Sophia Project houses were located. The full-time live-in community collectively maintained two large houses with beautiful gardens, created safe and beautiful homes and childcare environments, and were a positive force in the life of the neighborhood.

- Trained young adults through a vigorous program of professional development and service internships.

For the first years of the project I did most of the publicity and wrote the grant proposals. Through the fourteen years of the project, David provided the many required financial documents. In later years three part-time staff members took over many of the fundraising tasks.

Sophia Project would not have been successful in the essential work of fundraising without the help of the board of trustees, the board of advisors, and the many friends in Camphill, Waldorf Early Childhood Education, and other anthroposophical communities and institutions.

Also indispensable were the in-kind donations received from the handwork group and the Secret Santa Parents of the San Francisco Waldorf school, both organized by Sharry Wright. We also received generous donations of toys, household items, and food from many churches, organizations, and individuals. Weekly volunteers helped cook and garden; other occasional volunteers sewed curtains and helped paint. All these generous people understood it would not serve the children well to be attended by a stream of well-meaning but constantly changing volunteers. They were willing to do tasks that the live-in community could not do while working with the children.

Sophia Project
Agreement for an Internship in Service

What can you expect during the working day?

The work with children takes place in a nurturing, Waldorf-based nursery class, an infant-toddler program, before- and after-school programs, respite care weekends and through family support. Our childcare hours are determined in accordance with the needs of the families we serve. We are open from Monday to Friday, from 6:00 a.m. to 6:30 p.m. We provide transportation to and from home for some families.

There is a well-defined rhythm and form to the day, which maintains an orderly vitality in the environment, and nurtures security in the children. Within this framework there is room for flexibility in responding to the need of the moment. We expect interns to have the ability to work within our rhythms and activity forms. Rhythm carries us together through the day and creates safety for the children.

Between 6:00 a.m. and 6:30 p.m. Monday through Friday, you can expect to be working approximately seven hours with the children. During one of those hours the children will be taking a nap. You will sometimes prepare a warm lunch for up to 15 people. Often, the children need to be engaged with a staff person on a one-to-one basis. In addition you can expect to be cleaning or gardening for up to two hours within the 12-hour period. We clean the day care areas thoroughly every day. Hygiene is important because the children have weak immune systems and are prone to illness and infections.

Who will be supervising you?

The children's activities and schedules are organized by Carol Cole, Program Director. Carol is responsible for developing, guiding and supervising the work with children and the interns. As an intern you are expected to work with the children according to Carol's direction.

Relating with the mothers and families

You will have contact with the families and parents of children at Sophia House. Every step we make influences the child and the family. This ripple effect can encourage us because the healing work with a child is shared by the whole family. On the other hand, the mothers we work with are very vulnerable to criticism and feelings of shame, and it is easy to unwittingly undermine their confidence with an attitude, word or gesture, however well meant. Working with parents and responding to their needs and concerns requires experience and skills. We expect interns and volunteers to take direction from Carol in your relationships with family members. When asked by a parent for help, the appropriate approach is to listen respectfully, and to suggest to the person that she or he talk with Carol.

Respite care

Approximately every second weekend, the Sophia Project community welcomes children to stay for respite care. The children enjoy a nurturing and happy weekend while parents and caregivers of children at risk are given a much-needed break. This is a powerful child neglect and abuse prevention tool. We expect interns to be active in a care-giving role during respite weekends. This will probably include swimming, ice-skating, hiking, artistic work or some other activity done with the children. You have one day off that week, probably Sunday. We sometimes need to offer emergency respite care.

Weekend activities

On some respite weekends, Sophia Project provides activities for children of the neighborhood or art workshops for older children. These may include painting, gardening, doll making, etc. We expect interns to share responsibility for initiating, planning, preparing and offering an activity to local children. The neighborhood children also come for short, unscheduled play for 20 – 45 minutes from time to time during evenings and off weekends. We encourage this and share supervising them between us.

Professional supervision

As an intern, you will receive professional supervision every other week with Carol. This is an opportunity to raise questions and concerns about the children, learn about the ideas and principles that inform our work, and receive feedback and encouragement about your own progress.

Intern orientation

It can take a little time to orientate to the new environment, work schedule, rhythm of the day and week, the children and the community members. We try to support interns through this process so that it goes as smoothly as possible.

For the first few weeks, until you feel settled, a member of the house community will support you, checking in with you about your day and any questions or concerns you may have. You will also be introduced to your tasks and responsibilities in the household. Within a few days after your arrival, one of us will accompany you to the public transportation center and from then on you can move around independently. In the end of August, interns and coworkers have a formal five-day orientation. At first, interns can feel overwhelmed by the immensity of what the children and mothers have to bear in their everyday lives. This can be emotionally challenging in the first month of the internship.

Helping conversations: Processing

Working with people who have experienced trauma in their lives can trigger our own wounds and you may experience strong, unfamiliar feelings. Working closely with people who have experienced a lot of trauma, and living in a life sharing community, challenges us to get to know different parts of ourselves. As an intern you will have a monthly session with a trained counselor who will support you to process your internal feelings and reactions in a safe and empowering way.

Holding the needs of the children as your primary focus

The children who attend our programs have experienced a great deal of trauma in their lives, and are in need of healing. Sometimes, their behavior may feel hurtful to you. These behaviors are a reaction to painful past experiences that are locked in their bodies. They also are a result of difficult conditions in the physical and social environment and among the adults they live with (poverty, hunger, stress, hopelessness, rage, sadness, abuse, being socially devalued, unemployment, etc.). These behaviors are not about you; they are not meant as a personal attack although sometimes it can feel like that.

The same strong feelings may arise in you when you work with the children and mothers. Some people can find this overwhelming at times. Professional supervision is one way for you to develop greater awareness and ability to meet the needs of the children while coping with the feelings and reactions that they stir in you. Our experience is that the more you take up the learning and suggestions from your supervision and processing sessions, the greater confidence and competence you will develop with the children and handling your internal issues in a way that does not negatively impact your work.

One of the powerful healing tools that we practice at Sophia Project is to find within ourselves the quality that the child needs. For instance, we may need to help a child bring more lightness into her life and so we work on our own inner life to find a place of light within ourselves and bring this inner quality into our way of being and relating with the child.

Be the change you want to see in the world

— Gandhi[1]

Supporting you to do this work – what you can expect from us

In supporting you to become better assistants to the work of the project, Sophia Project provides:

Program meeting – weekly guidance in curriculum and child development

House meeting – alternate week practical, social and personal arrangements and needs

Artistic work – alternate week, one of the coworkers (interns and staff) leads the group in an artistic activity

Study group – weekly study and conversation about anthroposophical topics, inner work, and writings of people who inspire and inform our work or other interest of coworkers/interns

Supervision meeting with Carol – every other week individual guidance in work with the children and mothers

Processing meeting with counselor – a monthly helping conversation to work through internal feelings and reactions that arise through the work

Occasionally we find that for some individuals this is not enough support for them to function well as an intern with the children as their primary focus. Additional support might mean individual therapy, regular structured group process around interpersonal issues, additional time with the program director and a greater level of theoretical explanations. It is important that each intern understands that:

<u>We are not in position to provide more than outlined here.</u>

Our resources of time, energy, money, wisdom, must be primarily directed towards the direct needs of the children and mothers we serve. Although the additional needs of interns are understandable and valid, those who need a greater level of support than we currently offer are not suited to an internship-in-service at Sophia Project. It is important that you be as clear and honest with yourself and with us as possible about your own needs before joining us. If at any stage during your time here we feel this is a concern, we will approach you about it. Every three months there will be a time for evaluation of the internship. If after clarifying the difficulties and working out possible solutions an intern's work or attitude is not meeting the needs of the children, of the mothers, and of the project the internship may be terminated.

Learning Agreement

What do we hope interns will learn?

The social and educational challenges that face the children and families we support are complex. Sometimes the educational need of the young child and the social need of the family appear to be in conflict. For instance: the young child needs to have the freedom to explore the qualities of mud, water, grass and dirt. However if the child is dirty the mother may well be accused of not taking care of her child properly and she also has to deal with the practical barrier of not having laundry facilities readily available. At Sophia Project you are expected to learn to bear this tension of opposites in an imperfect world, while still supporting the young child and the family as best we can. This is a creative social art.

Internship in service at Sophia House and Myrtle House means learning by doing. To intern means to be on the inside of something, in this case, the inside of Sophia Project. We draw our strength and inspiration from the work of Rudolf Steiner and Karl König. The source of most learning for you as an intern will come through direct service to the children and families and by engaging in the experience of being a community member and practicing life sharing with others. Only some of that learning can be processed, examined in meetings, and the theory behind it fully explained. It will not be possible to process all of each person's learning in meetings. You may be accustomed to learning mainly through thinking. Here, we learn mainly by doing.

It is not an expectation on the part of Sophia Project – and it is not reasonable one on the part of the intern – to learn in eleven months all there is to know about these children, the mothers, the neighborhood, etc., and to be able to recreate it yourself the month after you leave; the experience does offer some very valuable learning. Sometimes, an intern may be doing a specific practicum with practical and theoretical components as one part of the experience. Then, in her role as practicum supervisor, Carol builds into this person's work responsibilities opportunities to put into practice ideas that he or she has already learned at school, reflect on them from a theoretical angle, and write them up.

It is not just the answers we are after but good questions. There will always be unanswered questions. We hope that as an intern you will leave with questions that you wish to continue pursuing – some well formed and some just bubbling to the surface.

Learning topics

This is an internship in service. It is important to understand that this is not a full early childhood education training course, nor will it provide answers to all social justice issues. You will have many opportunities to learn.

By the time you leave, we expect you to have learned about the following topics. We have graded the learning into three levels of result. By being an intern, you will naturally have exposure to these topics. The level of understanding that you acquire, and your ability to mold what you have experienced into a working tool that you can use after your time here in other settings, will depend largely on your active engagement in the opportunities offered here.

Topic	Exposure	Basic understanding	Working knowledge (tools)
Domestic violence	X		
Abuse and trauma: impact and indicators	X	X	
Impact of family life on child	X	X	X
Parenting issues	X	X	
Impact of social/economic environment on daily life of child	X	X	X
Modeling healthy/healing attitudes and habits in daily life	X	X	X
Forming and honoring social agreements	X	X	X
Study content	X	X	
Recognizing appropriate boundaries: place, time etc.	X	X	X
Processing experiences	X	X	
Anthroposophical view of human being	X	X	
Mission of Sophia Project	X	X	X

Topic	Exposure	Basic understanding	Working knowledge (tools)
Child observation/study	X	X	
Child development	X	X	
Inner work	X	X	
Journaling	X	X	
Living mindfully as a representative of Sophia Project in a socially and culturally diverse neighborhood and learning the signals that may put out inappropriate messages	X	X	X
Inner attitude/practice: "How can I be of service to the needs of the project," rather than "The project should change to accommodate my needs"	X	X	X
The background philosophy behind Sophia Project: integration of community and early childhood development	X	X	X

Early childhood education and child development

Much of our work with homeless children and children at risk focuses on early childhood education. Being with the children will raise many questions and the need to learn. We expect you to have an interest in developing your understanding of the educational curriculum of Rudolf Steiner, in which the image of the human being is held in its wholeness (body, soul and spirit weaving together). We expect you to be an active participant in collaborative learning, sometimes in formal study sessions and meetings and sometimes informally. By the time you leave, we expect that you will have developed a working understanding of:

- Stages of learning of the child
- Nutritional needs of the child
- General physical needs of the child
- How the Waldorf early childhood curriculum addresses the stages of development in a child

- Age-appropriate discipline
- Emotional needs of the child
- Role of the adult/teacher in the life of the child
- The twelve senses according to Steiner's human development theory
- Learning through imitation
- The social needs of the child
- Caring for the physical and social environment of the child
- Fantasy and imagination
- Impact on the child of the emotional environment created by the inner and outer attitudes and behavior of the adults
- Principles of early childhood curriculum
- Principles for successful before- and after-school programs
- Written materials for individual study and group discussion are available.

Learning Plan

Once you have settled in, we will ask you to develop a simple learning plan that you will monitor yourself. This means thinking about and writing down some learning goals that you would like to work with while you are here. We will help you think about ways you can work towards your goals, and the kind of assistance that may be useful. Sometimes goals can change. We will also review your progress with you from time to time. We expect you to process the goals related to the children during professional supervision.

If you are staying for a year, Sophia Project provides you with funds to take a class at a local university or equivalent.

Reflecting and reviewing

As an intern, your daily schedule will include down time when you are not working directly with the children but need to be nearby. We encourage you to take these opportunities to reflect on the events of your day, what has come up for you, do some reading, writing, etc. Doing without reflection tends to harden into routine. Reflecting and thinking all the time without doing, remain in the realm of abstract theories and ideas. We try to strike a balance between these polarities.

We expect you to be open to reviewing and evaluating how you are getting along, and receiving feedback. We may also review our work as a group, focusing on particular themes. Reviewing and evaluating our progress may happen in study sessions, professional supervision, house meetings, and group discussion.

Journaling

Keeping a daily journal is a useful tool for reflecting on experience. As an intern, we ask you to keep a learning journal to help you focus on your educational and personal development goals with the children and the community. The reflective process is usually enriched in the act of writing, but this can be complemented with other forms of expression suited to individual styles, such as drawing, painting, clay modeling etc.

Social Agreements

The living community

Just as the educational programs provide direct support for the children, the purpose of our life sharing community is to create a safe and healing container for the work and a supportive environment for us all as coworkers.

By living together we have many opportunities to support each other in relation to our experiences with the children. We try to create a real home, as a sheath that not only supports each other but the children and the mothers. The mothers and children will also need to learn over time, how to create their own sustaining relationships. Our attempts to create a home together, get along with each other, enjoy each other's company, celebrate and learn together is our way of practicing what we are educating the children and mothers to do. Each intern receives their own bedroom and all common spaces are shared.

Social relationships

As members of the life sharing community we are creating a sheath together into which the mothers and children can enter. We do this by striving to see the highest in one another, even if at times this is clouded. We may or may not become personal friends but the way we engage with one another, the social weather that we create, has a big impact on each other's moods and the children. The children soak up our moods like a sponge and work them right into their bodies.

So living and working in Sophia House and Myrtle House means willingness to work out interpersonal difficulties that may arise in a respectful, caring way. By watching the co-workers work together, the children and mothers learn cooperation and the possibility of trust in one another.

Lifestyle

The children and families we serve come from very low-income situations. Our lifestyle as coworkers is a simple one; even so, maintaining our collective lifestyle takes more resources than are available to our families. We must be careful that the gap between our need for resources of all kinds and the daily life of the families we support does not get too wide. We too, must live lightly.

The population we serve cannot contribute financially to their education, and so we do not have the luxury of more staff than are absolutely necessary for the daily running of the children's programs. Every person working and living here has a vital role to play in the integrity of the whole project.

The limited number of coworkers challenges us to develop our capacity for social awareness, noticing how we impact on each other, being mindful of each other's need for personal space and also companionship. We are attempting to create an environment in which we feel comfortable to enjoy ourselves, relax, offer assistance, negotiate our own needs and notice the needs of others.

We work out together how to arrange the practical running of the house, there is no "housemother" as such, we care for each other. We share household tasks such as cooking, cleaning, gardening, shopping etc. We also may create social and cultural opportunities that we enjoy. On occasions, program related duties and meetings may take place during down time and on weekends. Flexibility is required. We have a house meeting every other week.

Mealtimes and food

Our children come from situations where food can be scarce or where there is a lack of nutritious food. It takes time and patience to help them come to relatively healthy eating habits. Shared meals are an important part of the work and as an intern you will be preparing and eating some meals with the children. It is important that coworkers can support this with the children. Lunch is the main meal and there are five set menus during the week. Dinner is a lighter, shared meal. Mealtimes in our community are social occasions for conversation and taking an interest in each other. The cooking is shared. On Friday evenings we often order take-out. If the weekend is not respite care, we organize our own meals. Breakfast is individual.

Self-reliance

Within our working and living environment, every person is challenged to experience both one's potential and one's limitations. We are a small community of seven or eight adults. As an intern you will need to have inner resources for personal well being. You may not find the "perfect peer" at Sophia House.

Time off

During the day, it is not so easy to leave the house because of the needs of the children. The work environment is supportive and flexible, and where possible we accommodate each other's needs for time off and transport. Sophia Project follows the Oakland Public School system's calendar for days off during the school week. For example, on Dr. Martin Luther King, Jr. day or Cesar Chavez day Sophia Project is closed. Typically on non-respite care weeks, five evenings a week are free. You will generally have no work duties on every other weekend and are free to go away. When Sophia House offers respite care weekends, you can have one free day during the week, probably Sunday. It is up to you to arrange what you will do on your days off. We are close to San Francisco and Berkeley, which have urban facilities and cultural life. Many beautiful natural environments are also near by. Nature, culture and exercise are ways of regenerating and rejuvenating.

Learning together

You are expected to join our community study group. One evening a week, we gather to explore together some content related to community development and social questions in the light of anthroposophy. We may work with writings by inspiring people who can nourish our inner life and our work. Interns are encouraged to suggest and /or lead study topics or artistic activities.

Overnight visitors

We often host people who are connected with the project for several nights or weeks. We have limited capacity to accommodate your personal visitors. On the weekends when the children are not here, occasional one- or two-night stays are possible after coordinating with other members of the house community. During the summer break permanent staff are finishing up the last year and preparing for the next year. Although the children are not here, it is an active work time and not a time for visitors.

If you are staying for a year, and have a need to invite visitors, Christmas and Easter breaks are possible. It has however been our experience that it is healthier for interns to get away from this environment for a week or two.

In any case, please do not extend such invitations to your family and friends without prior discussion and agreement with Carol and David.

Driving

When the Sophia Project car is not being used for business, interns have access to it for reasonable personal use and when public transportation is not practical, by social arrangement with other community members. Personal use of the car is limited. For those coming from outside the United States, the state of California does not recognize international driver's licenses. To drive in this state you will need to have a California driver's license, which involves both a written and driving test.

Telephone

The Project will provide each intern with a $25 phone card each month. Any costs beyond that must be carried by the intern.

Clothing

We need to be mindful at all times that living in our neighborhood, we are representatives of Sophia Project, a children's service program. We ask that people dress modestly (for example, tee shirts not tank tops). When working with the children causal clothes but not too casual are appropriate (for example, no torn jeans, exposed bellies).

Stipend

You will receive $200 per month. This is intended to cover basic day-to-day expenses such as recreation, personal items, etc. You will receive $40 per month towards transportation cost (such as public transportation, gas for personal use of Sophia Project car). If you fulfill a year commitment, you will receive $1,000 at the end of your stay. You will need to budget independently for vacations and other needs.

Insurance

We provide health insurance for year-long interns.

Student Loans

We can provide some assistance with repayment of student loans for year-long interns.

Safety Policy

As an intern you must agree to Sophia Project Safety Policy, which provides safeguards for the vulnerable group of people we support. The policy strictly prohibits the use of firearms and drugs by interns, staff and volunteers. Sexual advances of any kind to the children or families we support, including neighborhood families will not be tolerated and will result in immediate termination. No consumption of alcohol is permitted when children are present.

You are required by law to be fingerprinted, to have child abuse index check. All people working with children in the state of California are mandated reporters of abuse. Immediately upon arrival you will need to get fingerprinted and fill out legal forms. You are also required by state law to have a TB test for working with children, and this too needs to happen once you arrive before starting work with the children.

Smoking

The houses are smoke free areas. Smoking is only permitted outside and when children are not present.

Making a decision

It has been our experience and the experience of the interns that it is best when an applicant has as clear a picture as possible of the life here before applying. We hope this document has answered many of your questions. If you have applied and been accepted as an intern this agreement must be signed by you as a final step of acceptance. Please feel free to contact us with questions or comments at any time.

With best wishes for a good working together in support of the children and mothers we serve,

Carol Cole and David Barlow
Directors
Sophia Project

Endnotes

1   While this quote is commonly attributed to Gandhi, it represents a popular summation of the following, which appears in *The Collected Works of Mahatma Gandhi*, published by the Indian government in 1964. "We but mirror the world. All the tendencies present in the outer world are to be found in the world of our body. If we could change ourselves, the tendencies in the world would also change. As a man changes his own nature, so does the attitude of the world change towards him. This is the divine mystery supreme. A wonderful thing it is and the source of our happiness. We need not wait to see what others do."

Aeppli, Willi. *The Care and Development of the Senses.* Forest Row, UK: Steiner Schools Fellowship in Great Britain, 1955.

Bamford, Christopher. *An Endless Trace: The Passionate Pursuit of Wisdom in the West.* New Paltz, NY: Codhill Press, 2003.Brazelton, T Berry and Stanley I. Greenspan. The Irreducible Needs of Children. Cambridge, MA: Da Capo Press, 2000.

Center on the Developing Child at Harvard University. *The Science of Resilience* (InBrief). Accessed at www.developingchild.harvard.edu. Center on the Developing Child at Harvard University. *A Science-Based Framework for Early Childhood Policy: Using Evidence to Improve Outcomes in Learning Behavior, and Health for Vulnerable Children.* Accessed at www.developingchild.harvard.edu.

Coles, Robert. *The Youngest Parents.* New York: W.W. Norton and Company, 1997.

Easton, Stuart. *Man and World in the Light of Anthroposophy.* Hudson, NY: Anthroposophic Press, 1989.

Gerber, Magda. *Dear Parent, Caring for Infants with Respect.* Los Angeles, CA: Resources for Infant Educators, 1998.

Jaffke, Freya. *Work and Play in Early Childhood.* Hudson, NY: Anthroposophic Press, 1986.

Jenkinson, Sally. *The Genius of Play.* Stroud, UK: Hawthorne Press, 2001.

Jones, Noragh. *In Search of Home.* Edinburgh: Floris Books, 1998.

King, Robert, Thomas Merton and Thich Nhat Hanh. *Engaged Spirituality in an Age of Globialzation.* New York: The Continuum Publishing Group, 2001.

Kohler, Henning. *Working with Anxious, Nervous, and Depressed Children.* Fair Oaks, CA: Association of Waldorf Schools of North America, 2013.

König, Karl. *Being Human.* Great Barrington, MA: Steiner Books, 1989.

König, Karl. *The Calendar of the Soul: A Commentary.* Edinburgh, UK: Floris Books, 2010

König, Karl. *The First Three Years.* Edinburgh, UK: Floris Books, 2004.

König, Karl. *The Human Soul.* Spring Valley, NY: Anthroposophic Press, 1973.

Koenig, Karl. "Leading Thoughts." *Karl Koenig Archive,* from "Camphill Letter," Föhrenbühl and Saint Prex, 1965. www.karl-koenig-archive.net/mission.htm.

Kozol, Jonathan. *Amazing Grace.* New York: Crown Publishers, 1995.

Kozol, Jonathan. *Savage Inequalities.* New York: Harper Perennial, 1992.

Lievegoed, Bernard. *Phases of Childhood.* Lewisville, NC: Gryphon House, 1987.

McAllen, Audrey. *Sleep.* Fair Oaks, CA: Rudolf Steiner College Press, 2004.

McDermott, Robert, ed. *The Essential Steiner.* Edinburgh: Floris Books, 1996.

Merton, Thomas. *Ghandi on Non-Violence.* New York: New Directions, 1964.

Meyerkort, Margret and Rudi Lissau. *The Challenge of the Will.* Fair Oaks, CA: Rudolf Steiner College Press, 2000.

Müller-Wiedemann, Hans. *Karl König,* Edinburgh: T.W.T Publications, 1996.

Patterson, Barbara and Pamela Bradley. *Beyond the Rainbow Bridge.* Amesbury, MA: Michaelmas Press, 2000.

Pietzner, Cornelius. *Candle on the Hill: Images of Camphill Life.* Edinburgh: Floris Books, 1990.

Progoff, Ira. *At a Journal Workshop: Writing to Access the Power of the Unconscious and Evoke Creative Ability.* New York: Penguin Putman, 1992.

Roberts, Elizabeth, and Elias Amidon, eds. *Life Verses.* New York: Harper Collins, 1996. Salter, Joan. *The Incarnating Child.* Stroud, UK: Hawthorne Press, 1987.

Schoorel, Edmund. *The First Seven Years: Physiology of Childhood.* Fair Oaks, CA: Rudolf Steiner College Press, 2004.

Soesman, Albert. *The Twelve Senses.* London: Rudolf Steiner Press, 1990.

Staley, Betty. *Soul Weaving.* Stroud, UK: Hawthorne Press, 1999.

Steiner, Rudolf. *Anthroposophy in Everyday Life.* Hudson, NY: Anthroposophic Press, 1995.

Steiner, Rudolf. *Balance in Teaching.* Spring Valley, NY: Mercury Press, 1990. Steiner, Rudolf. *The Child's Changing Consciousness.* Hudson, NY: Anthroposophic Press, 1996.

Steiner, Rudolf. *The Child's Changing Consciousness and Waldorf Education.* Hudson, NY: Anthroposophic Press, 1988.

Steiner, Rudolf. *The Cycle of the Year.* Spring Valley, NY: Anthroposophic Press, 1984.

Steiner, Rudolf. *The Education of the Child.* London, UK: Rudolf Steiner Press, 1965.

Steiner, Rudolf. *The Esoteric Aspect of the Social Question.* London: Rudolf Steiner Press, 2001.

Steiner, Rudolf. *How to Know Higher Worlds*. Great Barrington, MA: Anthroposophic Press, 1994.

Steiner, Rudolf. *Isis Mary Sophia: Her Mission and Ours.* Great Barrington, MA: SteinerBooks, 2003.

Steiner, Rudolf. *An Outline of Esoteric Science.* Hudson, NY: Anthroposophic Press, 1997.

Steiner, Rudolf. *Social and Antisocial Forces.* Spring Valley, NY: Mercury Press, 1982.

Steiner, Rudolf. *The Spiritual Foundation of Morality.* North Vancouver, Canada: Steiner Books Centre, 1961.

Steiner, Rudolf. *The Study of Man.* London: The Rudolf Steiner Press, 1966.

Steiner, Rudolf. *Theosophy.* Hudson, NY: Anthroposophic Press, 1994.

Steiner, Rudolf. *The Universal Human.* Hudson, NY: Anthroposophic Press, 1990.

Steiner, Rudolf, ed. Christopher Bamford. *Start Now*, Great Barrington, MA: Anthroposophic Press, 2004.

Strauss, Michaela. *Understanding Children's Drawings.* London: Rudolf Steiner Press, 1978.

Van Duin, Veronica. *Homemaking as a Social Art.* Forest Row, UK: Rudolf Steiner Press, 2000.

Washington, James, ed. *A Testament of Hope: Essential Writings and Speeches of Martin Luther King, Jr.* New York: Harper, 1986.

White, Burton. *The New First Three Years of Life.* New York: Simon & Schuster, 1995.

Zucchino, David. *Myth of the Welfare Queen.* New York: Scribner, 1997.

Sophia Project Child Development and Parent Functioning Indicator System

The Child Development and Parent Functioning Indicator System was created to gauge the effect of the Sophia Project, as described in Chapter 3, "Assessment," and in Part Two, "Gauging the Effect of the Sophia Project."

— ASSESSMENT STAGE —			— OUTCOME STAGE —		
Baseline Indicator *Purpose: Record of first impressions*	**2-Month Indicator** *Purpose: Record of an emerging picture*	**4-Month Indicator** *Purpose: Comprehensive assessment of child need status*	**18-Month Indicator** *Purpose: Early assessment of daily program effects*	**Phase 1 Completion** *Purpose: Assessment of changes during daily program*	**Outcome Measure (Phase 2 Completion)** *Purpose: Assessment of changes during active relationship*
Child 1: Physical Development Y/N. Are growth, motor skills, eye-hand coordination and sensory integration on track for age? Describe current limitations, potential problems.	Repeat baseline questions. Y/N. If no, describe issues for 4- month in-depth assessment. Describe changes. Are additional special methods needed?	Repeat baseline questions. Y/N. Growth and weight on track? Gross motor skills? Small motor skills? Hand-eye coordination? Able to focus? Other Physical issues? Special assessments or methods needed?	Repeat baseline questions. Y/N. If no, are there physical problems that are likely to: a) need continuous monitoring b) present life-long challenges? Description and plan.	Repeat baseline questions. Y/N. If no, are there physical problems that are likely to: a) need continuous monitoring b) present life-long challenges? Description and plan.	Repeat baseline questions. Y/N. Possible outcomes: Successful intervention Partially successful outcome No change: positive No change: negative Slippage

— ASSESSMENT STAGE —			— OUTCOME STAGE —		
Baseline Indicator	2-Month Indicator	4-Month Indicator	18-Month Indicator	Phase 1 Completion	Outcome Measure (Phase 2 Completion)
Child 2: Speech and Language Y/N. Are use of language, clarity of speech and willingness to communicate verbally on track for age? If not, describe current limitations and potential problems and any special methods to aid development. What languages does the child hear and use?	Repeat Baseline Questions Y/N. If no, describe issues for 4- month in depth assessment. Describe changes. Are additional special methods needed?	Repeat Baseline Questions Y/N. Use of language on track? Clarity of speech? Willingness to communicate verbally? Other speech and language issues? Special in depth assessments needed? Special methods?	Repeat Baseline Questions Y/N. If no, are there speech or language problems that are likely to: a) need continuous monitoring b) present life-long challenges? Description and plan.	Repeat Baseline Questions Y/N. If no, are there speech or language problems that are likely to: a) need continuous monitoring b) present life-long challenges? Description and plan.	Repeat Baseline Questions Y/N. If yes, and baseline was no, outcome = "successful developmental intervention." If no, but progress, outcome = "partially successful developmental intervention." If no progress, choose: "permanent disability," "failed intervention," or other and describe. (If baseline was yes, outcome is "no change.)

	— ASSESSMENT STAGE —		— OUTCOME STAGE —		
Baseline Indicator	2-Month Indicator	4-Month Indicator	18-Month Indicator	Phase 1 Completion	Outcome Measure (Phase 2 Completion)
Child 3: Play Y/N. Does child engage objects in play, play alone and with other children and SP caregivers in age-appropriate ways? Y/N. If not, describe current limitations and potential problems, and any special methods to aid development.	Repeat Baseline Questions Y/N. If no, describe issues for 4- month in depth assessment. Describe changes. Are additional special methods needed?	Repeat Baseline Questions Y/N. Play with objects on track? Play alone? Play with other children? Play with SP caregivers? Transitions? Lack of experiences in particular play realms, e.g. Fantasy, building or others? Other play issues? Special assessments needs? Special methods?	Repeat Baseline Questions Y/N. If no, are there underlying developmental, psychological or cognitive problems that are likely to: a) need further diagnostic attention and/ or continuous monitoring b) present life-long challenges? Description and plan.	Repeat Baseline Questions Y/N. If no, are there underlying developmental, psychological or cognitive problems that are likely to: a) need further diagnostic attention and/ or continuous monitoring b) present life-long challenges? Description and plan.	Repeat Baseline Questions Y/N. If yes, and baseline was no, outcome = "successful developmental intervention." If no, but progress, outcome = "partially successful developmental intervention." If no progress, choose: "permanent disability," "failed intervention," or other and describe. (If baseline was yes, outcome is "no change.")

— ASSESSMENT STAGE —			— OUTCOME STAGE —		
Baseline Indicator	2-Month Indicator	4-Month Indicator	18-Month Indicator	Phase 1 Completion	Outcome Measure (Phase 2 Completion)
Child 4: Social Interaction Y/N. Does the child relate to family members, other children, and SP caregivers in age-appropriate ways? If not, describe areas of disturbance and any special methods to help relationships develop.	Repeat Baseline Questions Y/N. If no describe areas of difficulty (peers, family etc.) and specific behaviors. Describe issues for 4-month in depth assessment. Are special methods needed to aid development?	Repeat Baseline Questions Y/N. Can child wait for a turn? Share? Does child demonstrate empathy? Relationships with family members appropriate? Relationships with other children? Relationships with SP caregivers? Relationships with others? Special assessments? Special methods?	Repeat Baseline Questions Y/N. If no, are there underlying developmental, psychological or cognitive problems that are likely to: a) need further diagnostic attention and/or continuous monitoring b) present life-long challenges? Are there family issues that need further attention with parent/s? Description and plan.	Repeat Baseline Questions Y/N. If no, are there underlying developmental, psychological or cognitive problems that are likely to: a) need further diagnostic attention and/or continuous monitoring b) present life-long challenges? Are there family issues that need further attention with parent/s? Description and plan.	Repeat Baseline Questions Y/N. If yes, and baseline was no, outcome = "successful developmental intervention." If no, but progress, outcome = "partially successful developmental intervention." If no progress, choose: "permanent disability," "failed intervention," or other and describe. (If baseline was yes, outcome is "no change.")

	ASSESSMENT STAGE		OUTCOME STAGE		
Baseline Indicator	2-Month Indicator	4-Month Indicator	18-Month Indicator	Phase 1 Completion	Outcome Measure (Phase 2 Completion)
Child 5: Psychological and Emotional Health Y/N. Does the child respond to change, frustration, surprises, and other potential sources of upset in age-appropriate ways? If not, describe extreme responses – especially withdrawn/ depressed, continuous crying, hyperactive, or enraged/angry. Responds to warmth and interest?	Repeat Baseline Questions Y/N. If not, describe extreme responses. changes since Baseline Assessment? Describe any special methods to aid progress toward equilibrium. What areas may need special attention at 4-month in depth assessment?	Repeat Baseline Questions Y/N. Are responses to potential sources of upset in the normal range of emotion for the child's age? Is there a normal, not excessive, number of upsets in a day or week? Is there a relatively limited range of stimuli – not global experience – that produces extreme reactions? Special assessments? Special methods?	Repeat Baseline Questions Y/N. If no, are there safety problems in the child's environment? Are there developmental, perception or other cognitive problems that are likely to: a) need further diagnostic attention and/ or continuous monitoring b) present life-long challenges? Are there family issues that need further attention with parent/s? Description and plan.	Repeat Baseline Questions Y/N. If no, are there continuing safety problems in the child's environment? Are there developmental, perception or other cognitive problems that are likely to: a) need further diagnostic attention and/ or continuous monitoring b) present life-long challenges? Are there family issues that need further attention with parent/s? Description and plan.	Repeat Baseline Questions Y/N. If yes, and baseline was no, outcome = "successful developmental intervention." If no, but progress, outcome = "partially successful developmental intervention." If no progress, choose: "permanent disability," "failed intervention," or other and describe. (If baseline was yes, outcome is "no change.")

— ASSESSMENT STAGE —			— OUTCOME STAGE —		
Baseline Indicator	2-Month Indicator	4-Month Indicator	18-Month Indicator	Phase 1 Completion	Outcome Measure (Phase 2 Completion)
Child 6: Safety, Stability and Belonging Y/N. Does the child show confidence in his/her place in the world, attachment to particular people, places and things, and no more than age-appropriate and situation-appropriate fearfulness? If not, describe areas of disturbance and any special methods to increase safety, security and belonging.	Repeat Baseline Questions Y/N. If not, describe areas of disturbance and any special methods to increase safety, security and belonging. What areas may need special attention at 4-month in depth assessment?	Repeat Baseline Questions Y/N. Are signs of fear appropriate to situations and the child's age? Does s/he participate in activities freely, move around in the SP spaces freely, use people's names, have special attachments in SP to other children or to adults, and anticipate what comes next in the day or week, as age appropriate? Special assessments? Special methods?	Repeat Baseline Questions Y/N. If no, are continuing actual safety and stability problems in the child's environment? Are there developmental, psychological, perception or other cognitive problems that are likely to: a) need further diagnostic attention and/ or continuous monitoring b) present life-long challenges? Are there family issues that need further attention with parent/s?	Repeat Baseline Questions Y/N. If no, are there continuing actual safety and stability problems in the child's environment? Are there developmental, psychological, perception or other cognitive problems that are likely to: a) need further diagnostic attention and/ or continuous monitoring b) present life-long challenges? Are there family issues that need further attention with parent/s? Describe and plan.	Repeat Baseline Questions Y/N. If yes, and baseline was no, outcome = "successful developmental intervention." If no, but progress, outcome = "partially successful developmental intervention." If no progress, choose: "permanent disability," "failed intervention," or other and describe. (If baseline was yes, outcome is "no change.")

ASSESSMENT STAGE			OUTCOME STAGE		
Baseline Indicator	2-Month Indicator	4-Month Indicator	18-Month Indicator	Phase 1 Completion	Outcome Measure (Phase 2 Completion)
Child 7: Connection to the Natural World and to the Arts and Culture Y/N. Does the child's history include any special connection to or experience with the natural world? Positive or negative? (describe.) Has the child had age-appropriate and mainstream experiences of the arts and culture? (describe)	Repeat Baseline Questions Y/N. If yes, describe special connections/ experiences not previously recorded in Baseline Indicators	Repeat Baseline Questions Y/N. If yes, describe special connections/ experiences not previously recorded.	Repeat Baseline Questions Y/N. The child has had experiences of arts, culture, and the natural world similar to counterparts from middle-class homes and communicates knowledgeably and confidently to other childre children, adults and teachers (if school-age) about these experiences. The child has "chosen" a mode of creative expression/ and formed an attachment to as aspect of the natural world that increases his or her sense of belonging. If yes, describe plan to support these interests.)	Repeat Baseline Questions Y/N. The child has had experiences of arts, culture, and the natural world similar to counterparts from middle-class homes and communicates knowledgeably and confidently to other childre children, adults and teachers (if school-age) about these experiences. The child has "chosen" a mode of creative expression/ and formed an attachment to as aspect of the natural world that increases his or her sense of belonging. If yes, describe plan to support these interests.)	Repeat Baseline Questions Y/N. If yes, and baseline was no, outcome = "successful developmental intervention." If no, but progress, outcome = "partially successful developmental intervention." If no progress, describe. (If baseline was yes, outcome is "no change.")

	— ASSESSMENT STAGE —			— OUTCOME STAGE —	
Baseline Indicator	**2-Month Indicator**	**4-Month Indicator**	**18-Month Indicator**	**Phase 1 Completion**	**Outcome Measure (Phase 2 Completion)**
Child 8: Cognitive Development Y/N. Through language, play, and adjustment to the SP rhythm, does the child show age-appropriate cognitive development? If not, describe current limitations and any special methods to aid development.	Repeat Baseline Questions Y/N. Describe changes since Baseline Assessment. What issues may need special attention at 4-month in depth assessment?	Repeat Baseline Questions Y/N. Is the child's speech and language use on track for his/her age? Play with objects? Physical coordination? Understanding of what is happening at SP? Attention to what's happening? Impulse control? Special assessments? Special methods?	Repeat Baseline Questions Y/N. If no, are there underlying psychological, emotional, or neurological problems interfering with the child's cognitive development? Are there cognitive issues that are likely to: a) need further diagnostic attention and/or continuous monitoring b) present life-long challenges? Are there family issues that need further attention with parent/s? Description and plan.	Repeat Baseline Questions Y/N. If no, are there underlying psychological, emotional, or other problems interfering with the child's cognitive development? Are there cognitive issues that are likely to: a) need further diagnostic attention and/or continuous monitoring b) present life-long challenges? Are there family issues that need further attention with parent/s? Description and plan.	Repeat Baseline Questions Y/N. If yes, and baseline was no, outcome = "successful developmental intervention." If no, but progress, outcome = "partially successful developmental intervention." If no progress, choose: "permanent disability," "failed intervention," or other and describe. (If baseline was yes, outcome is "no change.")

— ASSESSMENT STAGE —			— OUTCOME STAGE —		
Baseline Indicator	2-Month Indicator	4-Month Indicator	18-Month Indicator	Phase 1 Completion	Outcome Measure (Phase 2 Completion)
Child 9: Resilience Y/N. Does the child's functioning relative to the traumas of his/her early life show abilities for self-protection, problem-solving, hardiness and self-management? If yes, what areas are stronger and weaker?	Repeat Baseline Questions Y/N. If no, describe issues for 4-month in depth assessment and any special methods to increase resilience.	Repeat Baseline Questions Y/N. Does the child successfully ask for help when it is needed? Is s/he physically healthy most of the time? Can s/he bounce back? Can s/he take cues from the environment for problem-solving strategies that moderate frustration and improve self-management? Special assessments? Special methods?	Repeat 4 month Questions Y/N. If no, are there continuing issues of safety, security and belonging that need to be addressed? Are there cognitive development problems interfering with progress in problem-solving and self-management? Are there family issues that need further attention with parent/s? Description and plan.	Repeat 4 month Questions Y/N. If no, are there continuing issues of safety, security and belonging that need to be addressed? Are there cognitive development problems interfering with progress in problem-solving and self-management? Are there family issues that need further attention with parent/s? Description and plan.	Repeat 4 month Questions Y/N. If yes to all, and baseline was no, outcome = "successful developmental intervention." If no to some, but some progress, outcome = "partially successful developmental intervention." If no progress, describe. (If baseline was yes, outcome is either "some change" or "no change.")

— ASSESSMENT STAGE —			— OUTCOME STAGE —		
Baseline Indicator	2-Month Indicator	4-Month Indicator	18-Month Indicator	Phase 1 Completion	Outcome Measure (Phase 2 Completion)
Child 10: Imagination Y/N. Does the child demonstrate imaginative capacity and/ or engage in fantasy play in age appropriate ways? If not, describe current limitations.	Repeat Baseline Questions Y/N. If no, describe issues for 4-month in depth assessment and any special methods needed to develop imaginative capacity.	Repeat Baseline Questions Y/N. Does the child repeat stories told to him/her? Make up his/her own stories? Enter into fantasy play – not imitate what s/he has seen? Does s/he respond appropriately to imaginative exercises? If age-appropriate, can the child talk about himself/herself in the future. Special assessments? Special methods?	Repeat Baseline Questions Y/N. If no, are there underlying psychological, emotional, cognitive development, or other problems interfering with the child's imaginative capacity? Are there family issues that need further attention with parent/s? Describe and plan.	Repeat Baseline Questions Y/N. If no, are there underlying psychological, emotional, cognitive development, or other problems interfering with the child's imaginative capacity? Are there family issues that need further attention with parent/s? Description and plan.	Repeat Baseline Questions Y/N. If yes, and baseline was no, outcome = "successful developmental intervention." If no, but progress, outcome = "partially successful developmental intervention." If no progress, describe. (If baseline was yes, outcome is "no change.")

— ASSESSMENT STAGE —				— OUTCOME STAGE —	
Baseline Indicator	2-Month Indicator	4-Month Indicator	9-Month Indicator	Kindergarten Completion Outcome Measure	Kindergarten Completion Outcome Measure
Child 11: Kindergarten Readiness (age 4, turning 5 by enrollment) Y/N. Is the child ready to have a successful kindergarten experience based on his/ her cognitive, social and emotional development? If no, what are initially presenting issues that will need attention?	Repeat Baseline Questions Y/N. If no, describe issues for 4-month in depth assessment and any special methods needed to begin developing school readiness. What changes since baseline assessment?	Repeat Baseline Questions Y/N. Does the child understand the acts of reading and writing, even if s/he does not yet know letters or write his/ her name? Is s/he able to sit down and listen for 20 minutes at a stretch? Is s/he able to cooperate in and follow the rhythm of a classroom? Does s/he have age-appropriate self-management, especially emotional control? Special assessments? Special methods?	Repeat Baseline Questions Y/N. If no, are there psychological, emotional, cognitive development, or neurological problems interfering with the child's school readiness? Are there family issues that need further attention with parent/s? Description and plan.	Report child's kindergarten experience if enrolled Y/N. Did the child have a successful kindergarten experience? Will s/he be recommended for promotion to grade 1? Are there psychological, emotional, cognitive development, or neurological problems interfering with the child's kindergarten adjustment? Are there family issues that need further attention with parents?	Repeat Baseline Questions Possible outcomes: —Successful intervention —Partially successful outcome —No change: positive —No change: negative —Slippage

	ASSESSMENT STAGE		OUTCOME STAGE		
Baseline Indicator	2-Month Indicator	4-Month Indicator	18-Month Indicator	Phase 1 Completion	Outcome Measure (Phase 2 Completion)
Child 12: School Adjustment and Achievement (Age 6+) Y/N. Is the child's adjustment to school routines and expectations, and his/her achievement, in the normal range based on school report cards and/or conversations with teachers? If not, what are the issues that require attention?	Repeat Baseline Questions Y/N. If not, describe issues that continue to need attention. What changes, if any, have been observed since the Baseline indicators? Are any additional special methods needed to aid school adjustment and achievement? Issues for 4 month in depth assessment?	Repeat Baseline Questions Y/N. Is the child cooperative with teachers, courteous to other children, and able to sit and listen or focus on tasks as expected? Is s/he engaged in learning and making progress as expected? Has s/he mastered the chief skills needed for moving up? In what areas does s/he excel; in what areas are there learning issues? Does s/he enjoy and look forward to school – both the social and learning aspects? Special methods, assessments?	Repeat Baseline Questions Y/N. If not, are there psychological, emotional, cognitive development, or neurological problems interfering with the child's school adjustment and achievement? Are there family issues that need further attention with parent/s? Description and plan.	Repeat Baseline Questions Y/N. If not, are there are there psychological, emotional, cognitive development, or neurological problems interfering with the child's school adjustment and achievement? Are there family issues that need further attention with parent/s? Description and plan.	Repeat Baseline Questions Possible outcomes: —Successful Intervention —Partially successful intervention —No change: positive —No change: negative —Slippage

— ASSESSMENT STAGE —			— OUTCOME STAGE —		
Baseline Indicator	2-Month Indicator	4-Month Indicator	18-Month Indicator	Phase 1 Completion	Outcome Measure (Phase 2 Completion)
Parent 1: Housing Y/N. Does parent have housing that is safe, adequate for family care and comfort, and is likely to remain stable for at least 12 months? If no, what are plans to find better housing and/or stabilize housing arrangement?	Repeat Baseline Questions Y/N. If no, what are plans? What are issues for 4-month indicators that are likely to be affecting children?	Repeat Baseline Questions Y/N. Does parent have a lease agreement? For how long? Does parent have adequate income to meet rent obligations as well as other household expenses? Are there adults in the household not related to the children? Is the housing safe for children to move about and to play indoors and out-doors? Are there adequate space, heat, water, cooking facilities, beds and other furnishings? What are plans to provide extra care for children?	Repeat Baseline Questions Y/N. If not, what plans are needed to stabilize housing for this family?	Repeat Baseline Questions Y/N. If no, how is the unstable/ unsafe housing situation affecting the children? What are plans to improve safety, security, and stability? (Home visits at this point)	Repeat Baseline Questions Y/N. If yes, and baseline was no, outcome = "successful family intervention." If no, but progress, outcome = "partially successful family intervention." If no progress, describe. (If baseline was yes, outcome is "no change.")

— ASSESSMENT STAGE —			— OUTCOME STAGE —		
Baseline Indicator	2-Month Indicator	4-Month Indicator	18-Month Indicator	Phase 1 Completion	Outcome Measure (Phase 2 Completion)
Parent 2: Financial Viability Y/N. Does parent/s have adequate income to maintain housing and provide basics for children? If no, what are plans to address short-term financial viability of the family?	Repeat Baseline Questions Y/N. If no, what are issues for 4-month alert likely to be affecting the children? What are plans to improve family's long-term financial viability?	Repeat Baseline Questions Y/N. Does the parent have a job and/or adequate skills to get and keep a job that will support the family? Is the parent receiving public assistance? Is the parent receiving financial assistance from unrelated adult/s in the household; if so, how secure is this assistance? How safe is the assistance relationship for the children? What are plans for job-related education and training? How will housing, child care, etc., be sustained in the interim?	Repeat Baseline Questions Y/N. If no, how is the financial insecurity affecting the children? What are plans to improve long-term financial viability of the family?	Repeat Baseline Questions Y/N. If no, how is the financial insecurity affecting the children? What are plans to improve long-term financial viability of the family? (Home visits at this point)	Repeat Baseline Questions Y/N. If yes, and baseline was no, outcome = "successful family intervention." If no, but progress, outcome = "partially successful family intervention." If no progress, describe. (If baseline was yes, outcome is "no change.")

	— ASSESSMENT STAGE —			— OUTCOME STAGE —	
Baseline Indicator	2-Month Indicator	4-Month Indicator	18-Month Indicator	Phase 1 Completion	Outcome Measure (Phase 2 Completion)
Parent 3: Household Stability, Rhythm and Order Y/N. Does the child's home environment provide a predictable routine, relative calmness, and cleanliness and order? If no, what are the major obstacles to creating a home-based sense of stability, predictability and order for children?	Repeat Baseline Questions Y/N. If no, what are issues for 4-month alert likely to be affecting the children? What are plans to help parent/s create a home environment more conducive to healing child trauma and encouraging positive development?	Repeat Baseline Questions Y/N. Do children awaken, eat, come and go, and go to bed at the same times most days? Is the lifestyle of parent/s relatively free of conflict, shouting, loud music, blasting TV's and similar assaults on children's emotions and senses? Is the home well-kept and orderly? Do children have a sense of where things belong? If no, what are plans to help parent/s work on issues in the home environment that could be affecting children's development?	Repeat Baseline Questions Y/N. If no, how is the household disorder affecting the children? What are plans to improve stability, rhythm, and order in the children's home environment?	Repeat Baseline Questions Y/N. If no, how is the household disorder affecting the children? What are plans to improve stability, rhythm, and order in the children's home environment?	Repeat Baseline Questions Y/N. If yes, and baseline was no, outcome = "successful family intervention." If no, but progress, outcome = "partially successful family intervention." If no progress, describe. (If baseline was yes, outcome is "no change.")

— ASSESSMENT STAGE —			— OUTCOME STAGE —		
Baseline Indicator	2-Month Indicator	4-Month Indicator	18-Month Indicator	Phase 1 Completion	Outcome Measure (Phase 2 Completion)
Parent 4: Child Development Practices Y/N. Do parents have age-appropriate expectations for their children's behavior, make adjustments in these expectations based on the likely impact of unstable living arrangements, and use positive disciplinary approaches to help children align their behavior with expectations? If no, what are the key child development practices that need to be articulated, modeled and reinforced?	Repeat Baseline Questions Y/N. If no, what are issues for 4-month alert likely to be affecting the behavior and development of children during their time in daily activities at SP and what are plans to work with parents on child development issues?	Repeat Baseline Questions Y/N. How do parents speak to their children? Are they able to re-direct children from inappropriate behaviors? How do they offer protection and reassurance? Respond to upsets? Give guidance? Induce children to try new things? Encourage independence? Etc. (Home visit at this point.) What is the plan for promoting positive child development practices by parents?	Repeat Baseline Questions Y/N. If no, what are information needs of parents about child development – especially for their children – and how will these be met? What are child development practice monitoring plans?	Repeat Baseline Questions Y/N. If no, what are information needs of parents about child development – especially for their children – and how will these be met? What are child development practice monitoring plans?	Repeat Baseline Questions Y/N. If yes, and baseline was no, outcome = "successful family intervention." If no, but progress, outcome = "partially successful family intervention." If no progress, describe. (If baseline was yes, outcome is "no change.")

Other WECAN books you will enjoy...

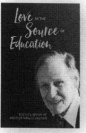

Love as the Source of Education: The Life Work of Helmut von Kügelgen
by Helmut von Kügelgen
Translated by Nina Kuettel, Astrid Schmitt-Stegman, and Cifford Venho
Edited by Susan Howard
Dr. Helmut von Kügelgen (1916-1998) was a champion of the Waldorf early childhood movement and a steadfast supporter of its growth in North America. In celebration of the centenary of his birth, we present this collection of articles, lectures, and essays to carry with us into the future, always keeping in mind his central theme: Love as the source of education. $14

Waldorf Early Childhood Education: An Introductory Reader
Edited by Shannon Honigblum
Here is a sampling of essays on a wide range of topics of interest to the Waldorf early childhood educator and to all caregivers of young children. This material has been selected from the rich array of publications created over the last thirty-five years by the Waldorf Early Childhood Association of North America, aiming to deepen our understanding of the young children in our care, and provide practical and artistic approaches to our work with them. $25

important part of early childhood work: the parent-child classroom or circle. With a wealth of warmth and compassion, teachers describe a variety of ways to welcome parents and families into the Waldorf early childhood setting and to show how these early experiences help create connections that last a lifetime. $14

Trust and Wonder: A Waldorf Approach to Caring for Infants and Toddlers
by Eldbjørg Gjessing Paulsen
What do infants and toddlers need from us?
This book speaks to the heart of our relationship as parents, educators, and caregivers to the child from birth to age three. Eldbjørg Paulsen has a wealth of experience as mother, grandmother, and Waldorf kindergarten teacher in Norway, and as a mentor, teacher trainer, and founder of a baby care project in South Africa. She offers insights into the child's process of becoming during this critical stage of development, and inspiration for adults who care for young children in a Waldorf setting and at home. $16

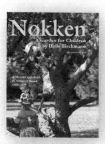

Nøkken: A Garden for Children, Second Edition
by Helle Heckmann
Since 1998, Helle Heckmann's description of a remarkable program for children from ages one to seven in Copenhagen, Denmark has been an inspiration for early childhood educators looking for ways to provide a healthy, nourishing environment for children in their care. WECAN is pleased to present this classic book in a new expanded edition. $18

Creating Connections: Perspectives on Parent-and-Child Work in Waldorf Early Childhood Education
Edited by Kimberly Lewis and Susan Weber
Spanning a range of topics and perspectives, this book is intended to help meet the need for more resources concerning a special and

store.waldorfearlychildhood.org

info@waldorfearlychildhood.org | (845) 352-1690